GW00458461

Maximise your Child's Happiness

A concise guide to protecting their mental health

Jennie Segar

Jennie Segar

Also in this series:

MAXIMISE YOUR CHILD'S PERFORMANCE

A CONCISE GUIDE TO UNLOCKING THEIR POTENTIAL

Jennie Segar

Copyright © 2023 Jennie Segar
All rights reserved.

Under no circumstances will any blame or legal responsibility be held against the publisher-author for any damages, reparation, or monetary loss due to the information contained within this book, either directly or indirectly.

Legal Notice

This book is copyright protected. It is only for personal use. No portion of this book may be reproduced, copied, distributed or adopted in any way, with the exception of certain activities permitted by applicable copyright laws, such as brief quotations in the context of a review or academic work. For permission to publish, distribute or otherwise reproduce this work, please get in touch with the author through her website: Jennie-Segar.co.uk

Disclaimer Notice

Please note that the information contained within this book is for educational and entertainment purposes only. All effort has been executed to present accurate, up-to-date, reliable, and complete information. No warranties of any kind are declared or implied. Readers acknowledge that the author is not engaged in rendering legal, financial, medical or professional advice. The content of this book has been derived from various sources. Please consult a licensed professional before attempting any techniques outlined in this book.

By reading this document, the reader agrees that under no circumstances is the author responsible for any direct or indirect losses incurred as a result of the use of the information contained within this document, including, but not limited to, errors, omissions, or inaccuracies.

This book is dedicated to my wonderful, resilient son, Alex.

About the Author

Jennie feels privileged to have worked with hundreds of children for three decades, employed as a primary, secondary and peripatetic teacher in schools and as a mum, tutor, nanny and governess in home environments. Having been lucky enough to travel all over the world, she has gained valuable insight into many different cultures and parenting techniques along the way. Qualified to teach both arts and sciences, she has been involved most recently in preparing students for the competitive system of private school entry in and around London.

Based on a lifetime of experience with children, Jennie brings together a comprehensive set of techniques, proven by scientific research to work, to help parents Maximise their Child's Happiness. As a parent, Jennie struggled to find a book that included proven methods she could employ to help build her own children's strengths, improve their resilience in tough times, and boost their happiness. This is the reason she wrote Maximise your Child's Happiness. If, like her, you want your children to grow up with confidence in themselves, an understanding of how special they are and a smile on their faces, then this is the book for you.

Jennie Segar

Contents

Jennie Segar

INTRODUCTION

It's weird; happiness is something we all seem to want for ourselves and our children but it's also something most of us struggle to define. There's the immediate delight of passing an exam, the pleasurable sensation when you bite into your favourite food and the warmth of a hug, which forces you to smile. These fabulous feelings remain with us briefly, but isn't happiness a little more lasting?

Happiness can be defined in many ways, which are all equally valid. In doing research for this book though, I've come to the conclusion that happiness comes from:

- being comfortable with who you are, knowing your abilities and understanding what values are important to you

- having the resilience and confidence to deal with difficulties in life as they arise

- being full of contentment with and gratitude for your situation in life, right now, in the moment.

Parents are in a fortunate position this century to have access to burgeoning research on the subject of happiness. There are books on many different topics such as journaling, mindfulness, social media and so on, related to finding happiness or protecting children's happiness and mental health. As a parent however, I myself simply didn't have time to read multiple books which delved deeply into different ideas and I was sometimes confused by the plethora of material available. I struggled to find a book bringing together practical advice and actionable activities based on solid, scientific research, which I could use to support my children and bring them happiness – that is the reason I wrote this book.

I want to give parents activities they can carry out with their children at home to maximise their children's happiness. Alongside specific recommendations, I have included a little bit of background on research carried out in each area, which supports the use of the techniques I discuss. I have cited the research papers I used for my investigations in the reference section at the end.

Family is everything and if you are reading this book, then perhaps you feel the same way. I dedicated my last book to Charlotte, my daughter, who worked so hard in her studies, Maximising her Performance all the way, and I'm dedicating this book to Alex, who took quite a few knocks in childhood but managed to come out the other end smiling and optimistic about his future.

I have divided this book up into three sections beginning with the letters H, U and G:

The H section is all about **H**ighlighting and building strengths. This includes activities children can do to understand themselves better and create a strong foundation from which to increase their happiness - boosting confidence, raising resilience and warding off stress along the way.

The U section is all about **U**nderstanding difficult topics - arming your children with information and suggesting approaches they could use in tricky situations.

The G section looks at activities your children can do to **G**ather happiness in the world around them, storing it away safely, ready to use whenever they need a pick-me-up.

I sincerely hope that this book will be useful to you in some way, wherever you happen to be on your parenting journey.

Jennie Segar

H HIGHLIGHT STRENGTHS

Real happiness comes from deep within us. We experience happiness when we feel comfortable with ourselves and loved just as we are, when we feel confident that we can handle day-to-day difficulties with ease, and when we engage in activities that truly utilise and develop our natural skills and abilities.

Many children don't appreciate what sort of person they are and often don't realise the incredible, natural strengths they possess – potentially powerful information for someone choosing subject options in higher education and usually something which is neglected until that point in a young person's life.

My first section here looks at the full spectrum of strengths and contains activities designed to help your child understand who they are and why they are special. They will build up a bank of strengths to give them confidence and a great outlook on life. They will learn what their natural, core strengths are, become aware of and appreciate the diverse strengths that people possess, and work on extending their grasp of several extremely beneficial strengths – those of optimism, gratitude and forgiveness. They will also learn a number of techniques, such as mindfulness, using affirmations and journaling, which will boost their minds and surround them with protection.

They will end up with a strong foundation upon which their happiness can grow.

List Strengths

Background

As human beings, we're all very different. For example, I have little patience when something goes wrong with my computer, so I am very grateful that my son is observant, loves learning the intricacies of a hard drive, and truly enjoys problem-solving. His core strengths are curiosity, persistence and a love of learning. Plus…he still has time for his Mum when her computer refuses to cooperate so he has patience and love as well :) Every single one of us has a range of core strengths and in life, if you can find a job which makes good use of these and also allows you to develop them further, then this is a recipe for success.

Children are born with core strengths and gain new ones as they mature. In my experience, though, they often don't appreciate that they even have these strengths unless someone points this out to them. As a teacher, I have witnessed first-hand how powerful it can be to point out to a child that they have a particular strength. One thing I learnt in teacher training many moons ago was that the best way to praise a child's work is to be specific - not just, "That's great, well done," but, "I love the way you contrasted the light and dark shades in your piece to make the image really stand out!" This sort of comment shows that you have carefully considered the child's work and it ends up being much more meaningful to them.

Children naturally want to fit in and find their place in a social group, sometimes struggling with the idea that it's actually a good thing for our society that we're all different. This is where activities that explore the idea of strengths can help children understand their place in the world and give them the confidence to be themselves, even if they happen to be a little different. It's good for them to see what qualities they possess, plus notice and appreciate strengths in others.

Research has been carried out exploring the effects of improving children's understanding of strengths. Specifically, many positive changes have been observed in children who have participated in interventions that educate them about strengths and help them discover their most developed strengths. It has been demonstrated that actively assisting children in identifying their own strengths and engaging them in tasks that help them understand what we mean by strengths, increases their self-esteem, improves their academic performance, and enhances their social skills. Overall, their happiness, well-being and life satisfaction have been shown to measurably increase. As a bonus, these interventions also provide children's mental health with a layer of protection against stress and lessen the likelihood of them experiencing psychological problems – building resilience.

Educating our children about strengths then is a valuable addition to our happiness toolkit, so what can we do at home to help our children benefit from this research?

In 2004, Peterson and Seligman first published their work, defining 24 character strengths and placing them into 6 categories. These are:

1. Wisdom and knowledge (creativity, open-mindedness, curiosity, perspective and a love of learning)

2. Courage (integrity, bravery, vitality and persistence)

3. Humanity (kindness, love and social skills)

4. Justice (fairness, leadership and citizenship)

5. Temperance (mercy, forgiveness, humility, self-regulation and prudence)

6. Transcendence (gratitude, appreciation of excellence and beauty, spirituality, humour and hope).

We all possess each of these, but we have a higher degree of some strengths than others. If you identify one of these as one of your core strengths, it means it comes naturally to you, you find this strength easy to employ and you enjoy using it. My number one strength is a love of learning, for example - I absolutely relish sitting down and reading non-fiction books, research papers and quirky novels. To many people, this activity might seem an extremely boring use of someone's time, but to me, it's sheer pleasure. If children can identify and understand what their core strengths are, it can help them recognise situations where their strengths are valuable, and perhaps seek out activities in which they know they will excel. Children should also learn that strengths can be developed with practice. By explaining this to your child, sewing the seed in their mind will make it more likely that they will actively work on improving their skill set, knowing that they can.

Action

In order to help your child tap into the benefits of strength training, they must, first of all, understand what each one means.

Part 1:

Go through the list of strengths with your child in any order, one by one. This may take some time since there is a lot of information to process. Ask them if they have experienced any situations where they have witnessed someone using a strength or a situation that could have gone better if someone had used a certain strength. Encourage them to identify any of their friends, family, teachers or people in the news who have shown that they possess any of the strengths discussed.

To help your child with this, here is a list of all 24 strengths with a short explanation for each and a suggested activity they could do to help develop that strength:

1. Kindness - doing things for other people without expecting anything in return makes them happy and often leads to them doing good deeds for us in return - both parties feel good as a result and everyone's mental health gets a hug. Is there a small act of kindness you could do this week for someone in your life? Hold the door open for someone you don't know, compliment a friend or offer to help someone. Notice how they react but also think about how this makes you feel inside afterwards.

2. Love - you show love by what you do and say to people who are close to you and with whom you share mutual trust. How would you show love to a close friend? Give someone close to you a hug and tell them what it is you like about them the most.

3. Gratitude - this is a very important strength that boosts happiness. Gratitude involves noticing and being thankful for other people's actions and all the good things we experience. Try to spot the next time someone does something good for you and go out of your way to thank them for this - perhaps make them a thank you card and deliver it to them personally.

4. Social skills - if you get on with other people easily and fit in, then you have this strength. Try saying hello to someone you don't normally talk to and ask them how their day is going.

5. Humour - laughter is very powerful, particularly in times of difficulty. Positive humour brings positive results and you have the ability to soothe and heal those around you if you possess this strength. Do some research and put together a set of jokes to tell to your friends or family when the opportunity arises.

6. Appreciation of beauty - this is an emotional reaction to wonderful things perceived by our senses - this can be something you hear as well as see. This strength gives people lovely, positive feelings and helps them to become less materialistic. Find three beautiful things the next time you go for a walk, produce something artistic yourself which brings pleasure or see if you can spot someone with an excellent skill or talent you can marvel at and enjoy.

7. Curiosity - this is an exciting strength, fuelling our minds to seek out new information. Why do things work in the way that they do? Find an interest, pursue it, become competent, and become confident. Do some research into something you are curious to know more about and find

out three interesting facts about it that you can share with someone close to you.

8. Creativity - its time to think a little differently, developing unique ideas to produce something new. This could be a work of art, a poem or story, or even an invention which solves a problem in a remarkable way. Try to identify a problem in your home and create an invention to fix the issue - it could be that you can't reach the bathroom cabinet, your light switch is too far from your bed, or your pencil case doesn't quite fit the stationery you have. Create a solution…

9. Love of learning - this has links to hope, curiosity and creativity and with it comes excitement and enthusiasm for the future. It's not about getting good grades, the pursuit of which can actually hinder you, but the journey of discovery. Identify a subject that really excites you to think about and see if you can find a library book on this topic or read some articles about it online.

10. Perspective - looking at a situation from another person's point of view or in a different way can help you make a better decision or change how you might react to it. If someone refuses to let you borrow their pen when you always lend them yours, this could make you slightly annoyed. Would your feelings change if you found out the

pen was the last gift given to your friend by their late grandmother, which is why they don't want to part with it? Think about the last time you had a disagreement with someone. Consider how you felt and then think about how the situation might seem to the person you had the disagreement with from their point of view. Try to understand why they reacted in the way that they did.

11. Open-mindedness - when you hear a point of view that is different from your own, do you listen carefully to this opinion and consider changing your mind? If you do then you could be open-minded. If you hear that a new student in school isn't very nice, would you wait to meet them and only then make up your own mind about them, or avoid them, just in case? Try to catch yourself the next time you are asked to do something new and you feel you wouldn't like it - notice what you are thinking about the new activity and try to take part with a clear, open mind rather than judging it before trying it.

12. Spirituality - if this is your strength, then you will have a strong feeling that life has a meaning or purpose. You feel that everyone in the world is important and there is something bigger than us. You may or may not be religious but you probably value love, gratitude and the beauty of this world. Spend 10 minutes sitting quietly

thinking about what you feel is the most important thing people should focus on in life.

13. Hope - looking forward to the future with a positive outlook requires hope. Creating goals and achieving them gives us great pleasure and spurs us on to create more. The world is full of opportunities. What would you like to achieve and by when? Having a vision, working towards goals and writing these down make them more likely to happen. Think of one enjoyable, achievable goal you would like to complete in the next few weeks. Write down your goal with a deadline date and make sure you complete it. Once done, think of another slightly harder goal and do the same.

14. Forgiveness - this is an important strength as it benefits our relationships with others but most importantly, helps us avoid harming ourselves. If others hurt our feelings, forgiveness is the choice to move forward, continue to behave well towards these people, and let go of any anger and resentment we might initially feel. The next time you feel hurt by someone's behaviour, notice the feeling and try choosing to forgive them and letting the situation go.

15. Humility - when a person who has the strength of humility succeeds, they don't show off their achievements but appreciate the efforts of those around them who helped

make it happen. People with humility accept their own shortcomings, take responsibility for their actions and never boast about their triumphs. A person with humility is quietly confident and open to the wisdom of others. Try to go a whole day without talking about yourself, asking others about themselves instead.

16. Self-regulation - could you go without technology for a week and read a book instead? Are you happy to say no to an unhealthy snack in order to enjoy your dinner more later on? Do you wait before responding and consider what to say when someone upsets you? Self-regulation is easy for some people but for others it is difficult. The good news is that it becomes easier the more you practise it, even if you work on it in an entirely unrelated situation. See if you can give up an unhealthy treat or game time for a day in favour of a more healthy snack or more productive activity. Think about how easy this was for you and try to do the same for double the time next time to build your self-regulation strength.

17. Prudence - this is all about making sensible, balanced decisions. A prudent person might be great at planning how they will prepare for trips away or exams; they will take time to consider their options before making decisions and will think before they speak. For one day, see if you can think before you speak in every situation.

Afterwards, consider how easy this was and if you think it made a difference to your interactions with others that day.

18. Leadership - if you have this strength, you are great at inspiring and organising people to get things done. You work hard alongside them, setting a good example, as well as encouraging others and noting any needs they may have. Some people naturally possess this strength, but many people need to learn how to be a good leader. Is there an initiative you could lead, such as supporting younger students at playtime, picking up litter in the playground at school or in the local community, or organising a book share scheme in your class?

19. Fairness - this involves sticking to the rules, treating everyone equally and looking at situations from a neutral standpoint. Is there anything at school or in the news which strikes you as having had an unfair outcome? What would have been a fairer solution? The next time you encounter a situation where someone is not treated fairly, think about whether it could have been resolved in a better way.

20. Citizenship - taking part in extracurricular activities, community projects and exercising some social responsibility all require the strength of citizenship. Perhaps you could join a scout group, do a sponsored bake

sale in school to raise money for a local charity or volunteer to read with younger children in your school.

21. Integrity - being honest, thinking about and sticking to values you hold as a person, being truthful, being authentic. Should you do what your friend is doing even if you know it to be wrong? Would you be tempted to pretend to be something you are not just to fit in? Think about your group of friends and consider if there are any actions or behaviours you do with them which don't feel completely comfortable to you and are not something you would do naturally.

22. Vitality - if this is your strength, you are full of enthusiasm and bring energy and excitement to your adventures in life. Identify something that excites you and see if you can arrange to do it more often or find out more about it. Eat a piece of fresh fruit and go on a short, zippy walk - these actions can immediately increase your energy levels.

23. Bravery - this is needed when you are afraid but still want to do the right thing. It might also be required when choosing not to do the wrong thing in a situation where your peers are egging you on. Bravery may also be needed when doing something challenging, like giving a presentation in front of the class or overcoming a fear of failure. The next time you need to carry out something you

are fearful of doing, remember that you are building this strength and need to exercise it in order for it to grow. Do some research and find a news story where someone showed bravery and courage. Try to imagine yourself in their shoes.

24. Persistence – the cliché is that becoming an expert in something takes 10,000 hours of practice – that's a lot of persistence. The most important inventions and scientific discoveries required dedication and persistence in order for them to succeed. As part of this, multiple failures, adjustments and revisions are necessary in order to master something. The rewards are there if you are persistent, even if you don't always reach your goals. Occasionally, it's a good idea to know when to give up on a goal - perhaps you can think of an instance when this might be the case? Think of a goal you would like to achieve, such as reading a book or learning to draw faces, for example. Push yourself to achieve your goal, practising again and again, if appropriate, until you succeed.

Part 2:

You might choose to do part 2 alongside your child - each of you should choose six core strengths from the list in Part 1, which you both feel you already possess quite naturally. Think about and discuss how you know you have each strength and pinpoint an occasion when you have made good use of it. Recording these strengths is great - your child could start a strengths scrapbook, with a double page for each strength. To make this more meaningful and memorable, encourage them to cut out and stick in photos or news articles to illustrate their strength. They might decide to create drawings or paintings or perhaps stick in physical items such as tree bark, packaging or feathers for example, which they feel represent their strength in some way. Each time they put one of their strengths into practice and it has a significant impact on them, encourage them to record it in some way in their scrapbook. Using core strengths should feel natural, easy and energising to your child; in time, they will find that they excel at any activity which draws upon one of their core strengths.

Part 3:

Put together a schedule that works for you - maybe this is something you do once a week on weekends, on the first day of each month or even during the school vacation. Choose a strength to work on that week/month, and ask your child to try to spot any situations when someone uses that particular strength. This could happen at home, in school or perhaps involve someone in a news story. Make a note of it and talk about it. Your child could record their findings in their strengths scrapbook or on a wall or fridge display to help them to remember what they found out. Encourage them to think about how they could learn to increase this strength themselves and perhaps see if they can think of an activity they could do during the week to help them learn to develop this strength. In the list in Part 1, there were some suggestions of activities your child could do for each strength. Perhaps use these ideas as a starting point, but feel free to come up with your own activities which could be carried out to help develop a particular strength.

Part 4:

After you have worked through your schedule of all 24 strengths, sit down with your child and ask them once again what they think their 6 core strengths are. Have there been any changes to their core strengths? Do they feel that any of their strengths have grown? Are there more strengths they feel they would like to add? Another use for their strengths scrapbook might be to record new skills they have learnt alongside this process - when setting goals for example - such as learning to spell perfectly for a test, juggling or doing a handstand, or mastering cooking macaroni cheese for dinner? Their scrapbook will become a wonderful record of all their strengths and achievements over time, and something you can both look back on and treasure.

Following this process, your child should have a greater sense of who they are and just how valuable they are. Children's strengths will change over time, so it's worth re-visiting these each year by perhaps repeating Part 4 of the process and adding a new list of 6 core strengths to your scrapbook or display each time.

Learn Gratitude

Background

I used to think that being grateful or thankful for things was something to do with religion. This was probably because I went to a school run by nuns for a few years, so memories of grace being said before dinner is part of my inner being - an act of 'thanking' God for liver and bacon casserole followed by sticky toffee pudding and custard. I have since changed my mind.

Incredibly, being grateful for the kindness shown to you, being grateful for your situation and experiences in life, or even being thankful for a delicious school dinner, can have a real, measurable effect on your physical and emotional well-being. There's extensive scientific research to prove it.

Research began in adults in the 1930s, but the wide range of benefits resulting from the emotion of gratitude were not discovered or fully appreciated until this century. In one early study, two groups of college students took part in a ten-week exercise - one group had to write down a list of things they were grateful for each week and the other group a list of hassles. Students in the grateful group felt happier, more positive and optimistic about life. They had better social interactions and even exercised more, plus they experienced fewer negative physical symptoms than the group asked to focus on their hassles. Other studies have found that people actively being grateful feel less pain and become less materialistic. Studies also revealed that the beneficial effects of an attitude of gratitude could be enhanced if participants expressed their gratitude directly to the other party involved.

After much study in adults, research with children followed and the findings from adult research were largely replicated. As well as the benefits seen in young adults taking part in research studies, children participating in studies also reported experiencing increased satisfaction with school. The benefits the children gained from participating in gratitude interventions lasted for several weeks after their study sessions ended. This shows that focusing on developing a grateful mindset, even if it's only for a short period of time, can make a difference in the long term.

Children have so much to learn about interacting with others and forming connections and friendships. Sometimes, things that might be obvious to an adult can be missed by a child who is still learning about the world. When one child goes out of their way to help a classmate, it is not always clear to the beneficiary that a kindness has been done for them. Children don't always appreciate what sacrifices other people make in order to carry out an act of kindness. Understanding this requires a bit of thought, time and life experience, as it's not always easy for a young person to see a situation from another person's point of view. Teaching children about gratitude involves helping children to appreciate when someone has been kind to them and helping them analyse what happened from all perspectives. Scientific evidence for the benefits of a grateful mindset is plentiful, so how can we help our children understand these ideas and develop one for themselves?

Education and practice are the keys to this treasure trove. In a study published in 2014, 120 8-10 year-olds took part in a week-long series of specially prepared lessons. Half of them were given lessons to help them understand about acts of kindness and gratitude. They learnt about what benefits might be gained from another person's deliberate, intentional actions and looked at what the cost might have been to their benefactor. They also explored the gratitude one might feel as a result. The other half of the children, the control group, received lessons with emotionally neutral content. In assessments conducted after the experiment, 60% of the control group demonstrated less emotional understanding of a situation where one person performed an act of kindness for another, compared to the group that received gratitude training. At the end of the study, an optional task was offered to participants - writing a thank you card to the school PTA. 80% more children from the gratitude group opted to write one. Following the success of the first study, the process was repeated over a longer period, giving children more time to practise what they had learnt. Beneficial effects were still measurable 5 months after lessons concluded. The children were essentially taught how to appreciate the positive intention of other people who do things to benefit them and therefore be grateful for these good deeds - broadening their emotional understanding and helping them see things they should be thankful for.

What all of the studies show is that having an awareness of the positive intentions of others and a feeling of gratitude towards them for this helps children be happier, improves their mental health, helps their social interactions, makes them enjoy school more and even positively affects their physical health - this is something we definitely need in our happiness toolbox. It doesn't come naturally to children necessarily though, but luckily, it can be learnt. So what could we do at home to promote a feeling of gratitude in our children and help them unlock all of these incredible benefits?

Action

Part 1

Talking to your children about situations where one person helps another will increase their awareness of acts of kindness and foster an appreciation of gratitude. Explain that when someone helps another person, they have a positive, purposeful intention to help, going out of their way to do something kind. Explain that there is a cost to them of doing this but they receive good feelings themselves as they can see the benefit of their actions for the person they help. Even if someone holds the door open for you, this potentially causes them a delay to their journey; if someone buys you a special gift, the cost to them will be in time spent choosing the gift and obtaining it, and possibly money. Educating your child about these concepts will increase their emotional understanding and encourage them to identify situations they come across in their day-to-day life for which they might feel thankful.

Not only could they begin to identify acts of kindness from others which they might be thankful for, but also start to notice wonderful experiences in this world which they are in a unique position to enjoy and be grateful for. These could be as diverse as seeing a magnificent sunset, experiencing the love of a pet or coming across a talented street performer on a shopping trip.

Part 2

To benefit from the power of gratitude, it is important to carry out positive actions on a regular basis that keep this strength in the forefront of your child's mind. There are various options for achieving this.

Encouraging your child to write in a daily gratitude diary would be fantastic but I do understand how busy we are as parents and this might be too much to include in an already complicated schedule. A weekly diary, filled in on a set day, may be a more manageable activity. There are other options, though. How about establishing a routine where each person in the family takes turns to say one thing they are grateful for that day over dinner, at bedtime or on the way to school? Alternatively, your child could use a wipeable board or laminated sheet hung on their wall to write down three things they are grateful for each week, filling it in on a Friday evening after school when there is a bit more time, perhaps. Whatever you decide to do, building a place for gratitude in your family schedule is a wonderful gift you can give to your child.

The potential rewards to your child from nurturing an understanding of gratitude definitely outweigh the small amount of time regularly needed to invest in this, and I do believe it's an important stepping stone to happiness.

Learn Optimism

Background

Optimism is a way of thinking really - if you are optimistic, you expect things to turn out well and have confidence in your ability to influence a positive outcome. It's more than this though, and also encompasses how someone reacts when things go wrong. Instead of feeling a sense of failure when something turns out badly, an optimist will see the situation as a mixture of things they did well and ones they could have done better. They will then use this experience as an opportunity to grow their skills, going out of their way to learn how to improve their performance next time with the belief that they can and will do better.

I was always impressed by the optimism of one of the students whose family I worked with for a number of years. When I began tutoring him, his academic performance was close to the bottom of his class. In tests, he frequently got the lowest grade, made obvious by the school including his position relative to the rest of the class on his reports. When his classmates came over on play dates, his generosity of spirit shone through as he praised his classmates' superior achievements in tests, musical abilities and sporting successes. He could have chosen to perceive his own performance as a failure in some way, saying to himself that he was incapable of doing well or lacking the necessary skills. He could have just given up trying. Instead, he saw every test as an opportunity to improve. Increasingly, he worked harder and harder and I still remember the day he came back from school with a massive grin on his face, having gained the top mark in his end-of-year exam in Biology. This was the start of a run of success for him.

A three-year study was carried out in Australia involving over 5000 students aged between 12 and 14. Their levels of optimism, thinking style, emotional problems and any issues with substance abuse were recorded beforehand and at regular intervals during the study. Students who were more optimistic about their futures were happier, and, incredibly, the likelihood of students exhibiting depressive symptoms was reduced by nearly a half for those in the most optimistic quarter of students as compared to the lowest quarter. Results supported the promotion of an optimistic thinking style for young people. Between genders, boys had lower rates of depression at all levels of optimism than girls, but the positive effect of optimistic thinking was the same for both overall. Somehow, optimistic thinking seems to protect young people from certain mental health risks, depression in particular. Other studies have shown that optimism is closely associated with academic, career and political success, plus better health in old age. You might well be thinking that that's all well and good if your child is an optimistic sort of person, but what if my child just isn't?

Before continuing, I'd just like to mention that there is a negative to optimism and it does have a slightly darker side. If you feel optimistic about everything, everything is going to turn out okay, so why not try something really risky? It will be fine, right? This sort of internal argument is one that would benefit from the wisdom that comes from the strengths of prudence and perspective. We must ensure that we encourage our children to be optimistic but, at the same time, continue to avoid things that could be rash or dangerous. Personally, this is definitely one of my tendencies, and I do need to remind myself of this occasionally, as I can get a little carried away with optimistic thinking...

Back to the positives of optimism, though, practising optimistic thinking makes children more resilient, more likely to see things through to the end and feel more confident and in control of their own destiny in the process. To answer my question above, luckily, this way of thinking is not something that is part of a child's inherent nature alone but a skill that can be learnt and nurtured. So, how might we help our children develop this important, uplifting and protective strength?

Action

Part 1

Lead by example. One of the most powerful ways to show our children how to be optimistic is to live this way ourselves. Having goals, milestones, and objectives to work towards, planning and looking forward to events, plus talking positively about the future are all ways in which we can demonstrate optimism. Almost more importantly, the way we handle more challenging situations provides another opportunity to show young people how to become more optimistic.

When something doesn't go according to plan, there are usually a number of factors at play which all contribute to the outcome. When I make a mistake, often my immediate, instinctive go-to inside my head is to blame myself fully for what has happened, dismissing other factors as I feel bad about it. "I'm such an idiot; why did I do that?" is a phrase that has passed through both my mouth and mind on more than one occasion. It would not be good to express out loud when trying to model optimistic behaviour, for sure. When I say something like this, I'm not being totally fair to myself either and it is not a thought process I'd want a young person to replicate. When speaking out loud, it is far better to say, "That didn't turn out as expected so I think I need to devise a way of making sure I do a better job next time." Young people notice what we say and how we phrase things and the subtle change here makes a huge difference to how they see us handling our mistakes. The message in the second way of phrasing it is that the task is just something we need to work on and is something we will be perfectly capable of mastering in the future. It's not a personal reflection of our lack of skills as an individual, as in the first example.

It is good to look at things from a wider perspective and come up with ideas about what could be done to improve the result next time. Some people are great at going straight to this; others, like me, need a moment to refocus and reset their thinking onto a more optimistic path. What's done is done and there's no point beating yourself up about it; all you can control is how you perform the next time you are in a similar position and make sure you learn all you can in the meantime to prepare for this, if appropriate to do so.

In everything that you do, try to be optimistic about achieving your goals. I've had a few rather intimidating job interviews with high-profile clients and have frequently felt unsure of myself, but I always push myself there with an expectancy that I will succeed. I haven't always, but I feel that those positions I wasn't offered would not have been a good fit for me - they were useful learning experiences, though, which helped me secure positions I did enjoy - an example of an optimistic way of viewing an outcome. I have had ups and downs with optimism but as long as we are aware of the importance of modelling our behaviour, hopefully, we end up with more ups than downs and can pass on some great habits to our children.

Part 2

Teach your children the importance of failure and how they can use it to their advantage. Last year I read a book by Matthew Syed in which he discusses different industries and how they approach failure - in particular, he looks at the airline industry, which has a culture of transparency about failures in the system. Employees are encouraged to report failures, which allows the industry to develop new procedures that improve safety. Syed contrasts this with the healthcare industry, where a culture of 'cover-up and continue' prevents safety issues from being identified and preventative procedures from being put in place. Failures happen, but the great thing is that we can use the experience of failure in a good way to create positive change.

The author also mentions two celebrity figures, David Beckham and James Dyson. He stresses that highly successful individuals like these didn't suddenly arrive on the scene with a plethora of skills to give to the world. Rather, they experimented very slowly, step by step, experienced thousands of small failures and eventually produced top-quality end results. Beckham kicked many a football in the wrong direction before managing to consistently send it where he intended it to go, and similarly, Dyson produced a stack of unsuitable prototypes before fine-tuning the successful product he is well known for the world over. For each, failure was intrinsic to success and very much part of the process - if success is the product, failure is the factory in which it is manufactured.

If a child can't draw a dog as well as their friend, they need to carry out some research, practise and learn how to draw a better picture of a dog. If they get a poor grade in a test, they need to experiment with different study methods next time to help them retain the information better and practise answering similar questions.

Each time your child experiences failure and struggles with negative feelings about it, help them to list things that contributed to the situation. If it was their performance in a test, for example, they might say that they're just bad at the subject, but try to pin down more precisely what went wrong. Perhaps they panicked and found it difficult to remember what they had revised. Maybe they forgot to have breakfast and were distracted by hunger and fatigue during the test, or possibly, they didn't allow themselves enough revision time in the weeks leading up to the test. All these specific issues can be addressed. If they missed a goal in a football match, precisely what practice could they do to help them increase their accuracy for the next match? Teaching them how to work out how to harness failure in order to produce positive results will empower them to become more optimistic and grow as individuals.

Part 3

Help your child take ownership of their optimism. Feeling positive about how things will turn out in the future doesn't happen overnight and children need to train their minds to think in this way. Encourage your child to think of a small, achievable goal which they would look forward to completing. Record the goal somewhere - perhaps on a notice board, the fridge or in a special notebook or journal. Examples of goals might be: saving up for a special game, learning how to make bread, learning how to draw anime characters, shooting ten hoops in a row, or getting full marks in their weekly spelling test.

Celebrate with your child when they achieve their goal and encourage them to come up with a new goal to work towards. Each time they reach their objective and experience success, their optimism will be strengthened and their confidence will have grown.

Part 4

Employ the worst-case scenario method in really tricky situations. Fear can very much grind away our happiness, potentially making us feel terrible inside and encouraging us to run away and retreat from the world. Children have limited experience to draw upon when confronted by troubling things such as failure, loss or confrontation with their peers and can find it difficult to rationalise situations or see the possibility of easier times or resolutions in their future. When things look bleak for them, it's great if they can talk about it with someone, but they may not always feel comfortable doing so. It would therefore be useful if they knew a technique they could use to help them process what they are feeling and increase their optimism going forward.

It can be good to turn around and face things we are afraid of head-on. Explain this to your child and then ask them to answer the following questions:

- What is the very worst thing which they fear might happen?
- Would they survive this?

- What would be the best outcome?
- What things could they do to move the outcome from the worst case to the best case?

Usually, when children confront the worst case that can happen in a given situation, their fear lessens and they can begin to see that they are still alive, the majority of things remain the same and the most precious people and pets in their lives are still there for them. Confronting and acknowledging fear can bring relief and allow an individual to see beyond the current difficulty, easing them back more quickly to an optimistic way of thinking.

Use Self-Affirmations

Background

Affirmations can mean many things. The general idea is that affirmations are words or acts which confirm to children that they are worthy, valuable and all they need to be, just as they are. Affirmations can be given naturally to children, such as when they achieve something big like winning an award, but it can also be present in smaller ways when, for example, one student sends a message to another to show they care, when a teacher pays a compliment to a child for using some great adjectives in their story or when your child sees the happy face of a younger student they have helped in the playground. In times of hardship, self-affirmations – affirmations in the form of short phrases or sentences recited by children themselves - can be used to help them see beyond their immediate situation and affirm that they have the ability to get through a difficult patch. Their resilience is bolstered by the use of self-affirmations and their confidence remains intact.

At first glance, this process might seem a little bit woolly and unbelievable, but what is actually going on in the brain when self-affirmation is practised is quite remarkable and there is scientific evidence to back it up.

Researchers who first looked into the use of self-affirmations by study participants realised they were having a positive effect. These results, however, didn't really pinpoint what was going on or the reason why participants might have felt some benefit from self-affirmations. Researchers relied heavily on a participant's own evaluation of how they felt following their involvement in studies. Because of this, a group of scientists decided to use functional magnetic resonance imaging (fMRI) technology to look inside participants' brains to see what exactly was going on when someone carried out a self-affirmation task.

The result of their investigation was published in 2015. Due to the nature of the technologies involved, participants were adults, but I feel that the findings are relevant, so I include them here. Sixty-seven adults took part and they were asked to rank their personal values in a list. The values were: creativity, relationships with family and friends, business, independence, living life to the full, religious beliefs, a sense of humour and politics. The adults chosen for the study were less active than average and considered sedentary, and it was hoped that self-affirmations might have an effect on their desire to take exercise so their physical activity was tracked. Whilst hooked up to an fMRI machine, half the group was asked to reflect on their highest value and the other half on the lowest. The group who carried out self-affirmations relating to their highest value saw positive behavioural changes in their physical activity. Nurturing and appreciating your strengths and values can positively impact your life in unrelated areas. Whilst in the fMRI, the scientists observed that neural activity in parts of the brain associated with self-processing and valuation increased. The researchers were able to demonstrate that self-affirmations produced measurable, physical responses in participants' brains, which in turn led to positive behavioural change.

In another study, over 500 students in the UK, aged between 11 and 14, took part in a study to see what difference self-affirmations make to academic performance. About 20% of them were eligible for free school meals - an indicator that they were from less wealthy, lower socioeconomic backgrounds. In the UK, there is data that shows that generally, children from lower socioeconomic backgrounds perform worse academically than those from more wealthy backgrounds. The students who took part completed three writing exercises over the course of one year.

Half of them performed self-affirmation exercises - writing about their values - and the other half did writing exercises based on a neutral topic. The self-affirmation exercises had a small impact on the children from higher socioeconomic backgrounds, increasing their academic performance and reducing stress levels to some degree, but the difference it made to the students from less affluent backgrounds was startling - not only were their levels of stress reduced but the academic attainment gap which existed between students in lower and higher socioeconomic bands was reduced by 62%.

As well as improving academic performance, self-affirmations have been shown to decrease stress levels, increase happiness and make individuals more open to behaviour change - all things we would like for our children. In life, though, naturally occurring affirmations from the wider world may come to our children infrequently, sporadically or be absent just when needed in a crisis. Wouldn't it be great if children could create their own self-affirmations which would be available whenever they needed them, allowing them to tap into this great resource on purpose and all by themselves? Absolutely, yes, and there are a number of ways of doing it, depending on their age.

Action

Part 1

For younger children aged between 1-5, the best way to help them benefit from self-affirmations is by deciding on short affirmations that resonate with your child, reading them out loud to your child, and asking them to repeat the words. It is never too late to begin using self-affirmations, but if younger children are encouraged to form a habit of using self-affirmation, it will help them in their future to lead happier lives with more resilience.

For this age group, simple statements are great for self-affirmations and will make a difference. Here are a few examples, but every child is different with unique qualities and values, so do be creative with the affirmations you use and help your child to take ownership of their values by choosing ones that have a special meaning for them:

- I am loved
- I am special
- I am creative
- My body is beautiful
- I am in a ball of happiness
- I am brave
- I am confident

Write each self-affirmation your child chooses on something like a post-it note, book mark or wipeable board. They might like to see a picture which represents their value alongside the words. They could perhaps draw the picture to make it more meaningful and remind them of their value or you could search online for a pictorial representation of the value and create something you could print off, colour in, cut out and use. For example, "I am brave" might be represented by a picture of a lion, ski jumper or firefighter beside the words.

Display your child's affirmations in prominent, much-frequented positions in their environment. For example, my preference is on the bathroom mirror so that self-affirmations can be said out loud first thing in the morning and last thing at night when your child brushes their teeth. Another popular option is to display self-affirmations on the fridge door.

Encourage your child each day to repeat after you their self-affirmation every time they are in the bathroom or kitchen, if this is where you have their words and pictures displayed. Whenever you feel appropriate to do so, revisit your child's self-affirmations with them to see if there was another one you could add or swap in if they have a new value they feel is important to them.

Simply saying those words on a regular basis will make a difference to your child.

Part 2

For children between the ages of 5 and 10, encourage them to write down their choice of self-affirmations and, once again, display them somewhere prominent in their environment. These statements can be more detailed and involved. Including self-drawn pictures would be great, too, as this encourages ownership. Here are a few examples, but it is important that they are chosen by and specific to your child:

- I am in control of my happiness
- I am strong enough to achieve great things
- I learn from failure and use it to improve
- I keep trying when the going gets tough
- My brain and body are powerful assets
- I enjoy a challenge
- I am loved and valued by my friends and family
- I work hard and am valued by my teachers
- I am kind to myself
- I am proud of myself and what I have achieved
- I am great at drawing
- My body and mind are strong and beautiful

Part 3

For older children, and indeed adults, self-affirmations can be longer, like mini paragraphs for each. Once again, display these somewhere your child will see them on a regular basis and encourage them to read them in their head or aloud daily. Perhaps, begin with three self-affirmations. In research studies, the self-affirmations that participants created were revisited and revised several times per year - keeping the original self-affirmations, changing some of them and adding some new ones as appropriate. Once your child has created a few, perhaps encourage them to revise them towards the end of every school holiday, to give your child a boost before each school term begins.

Here are a couple of examples to get you started:

- Being creative is very important to me. I really love to design and build useful things for myself, my friends and my family to use at home and in school.

- I am grateful that my parents love me whether I pass or fail, win or lose - they love me no matter what. Even though I sometimes argue with them, I'm grateful for their calm, thoughtful presence. They are my rock.

The examples I have given will get your child started, but if you want more inspiration for self-affirmations, there are many ideas out there if you search online. The main thing is to have a go and get started – it really does make a difference.

Learn Mindfulness

Background

I use mindfulness myself, almost on a daily basis, and include a version of it in my pre-exam spiel with the students I teach. The reason I do this is to help my students to be ready and able to do their best in assessments. When you were a child in an exam situation, did you ever look at a question on a topic you had thoroughly revised and your mind went completely blank? I certainly did, and have since discovered something that stops this from happening - mindfulness is the key to unlocking those elusive memories, but this is just the tip of the iceberg regarding the benefits to our children of practising mindfulness techniques.

Using mindfulness involves focusing attention on the present moment without analysis or judgement, just acceptance. Learning to use mindfulness is about developing your ability to keep your thoughts trained on what's happening now, increasing your awareness of what is going on both inside and outside your body. Children do this quite naturally at a young age - they can cry about one thing and a minute later be laughing about something else. Older children, however, take on board concerns and worries, analysing the past and worrying about future events. This can take away their happiness and even cause them physical harm if it happens over a prolonged period.

Certain regions of our brains develop the fastest when we are children. Ideally, we would like our children during their childhood to develop the ability to easily: learn new skills, memorise information, solve problems, concentrate on a task, see things through, look at situations from different perspectives and regulate their emotions. Various regions of our brains are activated when our children are developing their skills in these areas. The more a region in our brain is activated, the larger and more efficient it becomes, making tasks which use that region of the brain easier over time. Mindfulness activities have been shown to positively affect such useful regions of the brain.

A small study was carried out with adults looking at the impact of a mindfulness-based stress reduction program. This took place over an eight-week period, with participants attending weekly group meetings plus a full day and 45-minute exercises to do at home in between. Tasks consisted of mindfulness exercises that helped participants become more aware of their bodies, concentrate on their breath and increase their awareness of things they could sense around them. Their brains were scanned before and after the program and it was found that the grey matter had increased significantly in areas of the brain associated with emotional regulation, learning and memory processes, self-referential processing and seeing things from another perspective. It is pretty extraordinary that in only eight weeks, there were measurable differences in the brains of participants in these 'useful' regions. You might be thinking that 45 minutes per day plus longer exercises over the course of eight weeks would be hard to fit into your already bust schedule, so I can reassure you at this point that there have been studies that show meaningful results in far less time. Also, you can try interventions at home with your child that are fun and can be incorporated into daily life quite easily. The next study I'm going to discuss was only short, but its benefits continued to be experienced by participants when they were tested months later.

There is another region of the brain that is affected by mindfulness training, and this one actually reduces in size. When we are stressed, a part of the brain called the amygdala gets involved. The amygdala sets off a process that gets our bodies ready to react to danger. Our heart beats faster, ready to move blood to our muscles and help us run, we take in more oxygen, ready to give our muscles energy and make our brains more alert, and our blood is flooded with glucose to fuel our actions. Adrenaline and cortisol are also released. This reaction is important, of course, if we need to jump out of the way of a car or rampaging bull, but not really so great if we are stressed about the exam, which starts in a few minutes. When our bodies move into this 'fight or flight' mode, resources are moved away from parts of the brain associated with problem-solving or memory retrieval. This is the opposite of what we need our bodies to do in an exam situation. It is still an important response, but in today's world, we experience many triggers which set this system off inappropriately and it can be difficult to bring your body out of this state, reducing activity in the amygdala and increasing activity in other parts of the brain when you need it most - evolution was left behind a little on this one I feel.

Luckily for us, studies in adults have shown that practising mindfulness techniques have the effect of altering the structure and function of the amygdala. A group of unemployed participants were recruited in Pittsburgh, PA; they all showed existing signs of stress. One half went on a general three-day health retreat and the other half underwent a three-day mindfulness program, which included body scanning (see Part 2 below), mindful eating (see Part 4 below) and mindful movement exercises. Their brains were scanned and hair samples were taken to test for cortisol levels before the intervention and four months later. Results confirmed that, even after only a few days of mindfulness training, the structure and function of the amygdala was reduced compared to the control group of participants, meaning that those taking part in this intervention experienced corresponding reduced levels of stress. One of the exercises used in mindfulness training is to concentrate on the breath. When you breathe deeply, using your diaphragm, signals are sent to your brain to close down the stress response and relax, reversing the effects of the amygdala. Shallow breaths are needed for fight or flight and are kick-started by the amygdala and deep breaths, particularly ones with a longer outwards breath, bring you back to a state of calm once more.

Few studies on the effects of mindfulness in children have involved brain scans, but have measured changes in mood, stress levels, anxiety, wellbeing and happiness; the results tally with those found in adults. Mindfulness training has been shown to increase children's emotional regulation and overall life satisfaction. A 2018 review of research findings published to date on the effectiveness of mindfulness training with children highlighted its many benefits. As well as helping children with emotional regulation, behaviour and mood, studies found that mindfulness interventions even improved children's physical well-being and academic grades. All good stuff, so it's time to take a look at how we can bring this practice into our children's lives so that they can tap into this surprising and amazing resource.

Action

These exercises can be done by your child alone, but they will initially need to be shown what to do. Have a go yourself, then you will be able to describe the process more easily to your child. You could do the exercise together or alternatively, sometimes children like to tell someone what they notice whilst carrying out mindful exercises, so you could fulfil the role of sounding board for them until they get used to the technique. I benefit from doing mindful exercises myself, as do many adults, and your child will benefit from your example if you choose to practise these exercises together.

Part 1

Deep breathing. This is a great one to draw upon when you are waiting to go into an exam or even sitting at your desk waiting to turn over the paper – in this case, just do the breathing from step 4. It can be done anywhere and in any position when you are either stationary or moving slowly, with or without the cuddly toy, which is just used to encourage those deep breaths.

1. In order to learn how it works, lie on the sofa with a comfy pillow under your head and knees if you need to.

2. Place a small cuddly toy on top of your tummy and watch it rise and fall as you breathe in and out, making sure it stays on top. This can be a little tricky.

3. Focus on the toy and imagine you are filling a balloon each time you breathe in and emptying it each time you breathe out. You are giving your toy a roller coaster ride!

4. Slow your breathing and practise counting steadily as you breathe - maybe you can count to 5 as you breathe in and then count to 5 at the same speed as you breathe out. Each time you breathe in, start at 1, then start at 1 again for the breath out.

5. Breathe in whilst counting slowly. You might get to number 5, 10 or even more, depending on how relaxed you now feel.

6. When you have breathed in fully, try holding your breath for 2 counts.

7. Breathe out whilst counting and see if you can get to a higher number than you breathed in. For example, if you breathed in for 5, held for 2 then try to breathe out for 7.

8. Repeat the process a few times and notice what numbers you reached.

9. If you lose count, notice this, accept it and then just return to counting and breathing once more. Similarly, if your mind wanders, notice it, accept it and bring your mind back to counting and breathing again.

10. When you feel relaxed and comfortable, stop counting and notice how you feel - better, calmer, sleepy, alert. Just notice it and let it go.

Part 2

Body scanning. Again, this can be done anywhere but it might be best to practise this at home whilst sitting somewhere familiar to begin with. It might be worth talking through different parts of the exercise with your child the first few times, like a guided meditation, and they could tell you out loud how they feel.

Eventually, they will know the process and be able to follow it themselves.

1. Sit on a comfortable chair, sofa or even lie in bed.

2. Starting with your head, notice the air going into and out of your nose. How does it feel inside your nose and as it passes over your body? Does your hair tickle your face at all and are the muscles in your face relaxed or tense? If your head touches a headrest, where does it touch and how does it feel? If your child finds it useful whilst they are learning to do this, they could tell you out loud what they feel.

3. If you find that your mind begins to wander, notice this and bring it back to observing your body once more. This part of the process is very powerful - the more you train your mind to come back, the stronger you become.

4. Move on to the next part of your body - your shoulders, arms and hands. What are they touching? Can you feel where you make contact with the chair? Can you feel your breath pass over them?

5. Do the same with your back, bottom, legs and feet. Notice the smallest details that you can about how your body feels, what it connects with and if those parts of the body are comfortable or not. Notice these things, then let them go and move on.

This exercise can be done anywhere - at home, whilst lying on the beach, under a tree, or even on the tube. It brings you back to thinking in the moment and being really aware of your own body.

Part 3

Mindfulness in nature. Again, this exercise can be done anywhere too, but it needs to be practised somewhere familiar first. I often do this when I'm on a walk in the hills as I like to feel connected to my surroundings and enjoy noticing small changes in nature throughout the year.

1. Find somewhere comfortable to sit outside - somewhere in nature or perhaps in a garden - and begin breathing slowly and steadily.

2. What can you hear and how would you describe it? Is it loud or soft, high or low, raspy or smooth? What other sounds can you hear? Is there an animal or insect rustling around nearby? Notice any sounds and let them go.

3. If you find your mind wanders, notice this, don't judge yourself for it and just bring it back to thinking about the things you can sense around you. Remember that every time your mind wanders and you bring it back, you become stronger.

4. What can you smell? Anything or nothing? How would you describe any smells? Notice them and let them go.

5. What can you see around you? How would you describe the colours? What are the plants like? Notice them and let them go.

Did you perhaps notice something you would otherwise have missed?

Part 4

Mindful eating. You are going to be a food detective. This is quite fun and is best done with someone else so that you can compare notes. It is sometimes surprising!

1. Choose a small food item that you normally eat. For example, a radish, raisin, grape, strawberry or cherry tomato.

2. Study your food, noticing the outside. Is it shiny, smooth, rough, a vibrant colour? How would you describe it? How does it feel - cold, warm, soft, rough, sticky?

3. Put it in your mouth and feel it against your tongue. How does it feel and what does it taste like at first?

4. Crunch down on it and notice how the flavour develops. Has the taste changed? How does it feel against your tongue now?

5. Swallow the food, noticing how your mouth moves to push the food down. Can you feel it as it moves down your throat?

Afterwards, discuss with each other what you now think about that food. Was this exercise any different from how you normally experience this food?

Learn Forgiveness

Background

Forgiveness is a skill that can be quite difficult to master. It is a decision to overcome and let go of the pain caused by someone else and it can take some time to be truly granted. Forgiveness can happen openly when someone says they forgive someone else, but it can also happen quietly, within one's own mind, a choice to let go of the hurt and move on. Forgiveness does not mean forgetting an incident or telling yourself that your feelings towards the other person as a result of an incident are wrong; it's simply a choice to be compassionate towards the perpetrator, forgive their actions and free yourself from any anger and resentment you may feel.

I've struggled with this one over the years and have experienced first hand the damage it can do. When I was a child, I wish someone had explained my feelings and given me a method of dealing with unkind, thoughtless behaviour; peer group friendships would have been much easier for me to maintain. Unfortunately, the method I chose to use to deal with problems with peers was to detach myself from anyone who hurt me, which only resulted in me losing out.

It didn't help that I had an extremely turbulent childhood, due to the actions of both my mother and step mother. I have now totally forgiven them both. My mother had an appalling time throughout her life, suffering at the hands of her parents and siblings. In comparison, I have had some wonderful experiences in my own life and I choose to see that the cruelty I endured as a small child contributed to making me strong, resilient and enormously compassionate towards children, which is a strength I've made a career out of. I know my mother must have loved me deep down and regretted her actions and I just wish she could have had a better life herself. As a teenager, I was churned up inside by a feeling that I was unloved and unwanted by my mother, but over time I began to have empathy for the terrible experiences she had suffered, and I started to have deep compassion for her and an understanding of her situation. What she did was wrong but I have let go of any anger I felt towards her, choosing instead to forgive her and harbour only kind feelings towards her instead, tinged with some sadness for how much better things could have been for us all.

As I found out, when a child is subject to an offence, feelings of hurt and anger can result and a desire for revenge may begin to brew. In the long run, these feelings can grow and make it difficult for the child experiencing them to maintain relationships with their peers. Being unable to process these feelings and find a way forward has been shown to lead to consequences such as depression and anxiety and ultimately, like me, the one who has been wronged will lose out. The reverse is true. Suppose children are given education about the feelings they experience, provided with guidance on how to look at things from other people's perspectives, and are introduced to a method of processing these feelings and dealing with the situation going forward. Increased understanding of this sort reduces anxiety, builds self-esteem, improves children's wellbeing and makes children more empathetic friends.

A study was carried out on a group of children aged 11-12 in Hong Kong who had each been the subject of an offence and, importantly, stated that they had not forgiven the perpetrator. Over the course of two months, half the group had eight sessions educating them about the process of forgiveness and the other half had instruction about other personal development topics. Participants' levels of self-esteem, hope and depression were measured prior to the sessions, at the end of them and three months after the sessions had been completed. The results for children in the control group didn't particularly change when measured at all three points, but for the group who received the forgiveness intervention program, there were significant improvements at the end of the study, which remained even after a further three months beyond the completion of the forgiveness intervention program. Children's levels of hope and self-esteem were raised and feelings of depression were lowered. The researchers also recorded some qualitative results from the children's own descriptions of what they had learnt. It seemed that children who did the forgiveness training learnt to appreciate that people can't always avoid making mistakes and it's good to try to see things from their offender's perspective, using empathy and compassion when looking at what they had done. The children also saw that ultimately, forgiveness is a gift we give ourselves, helping both us and our offenders find peace and happiness.

Being able to forgive helps children to build long-lasting friendships and having strong personal relationships and friendships in itself can have a significant impact on a person's life.

In 1937, two rather inventive academics embarked upon the study of a group of young men from a mixture of socioeconomic backgrounds - some were busy studying at one of the most prestigious academic institutions in America, Harvard, whereas others lived in relative poverty nearby, in Boston. Incredibly, the health, happiness and wellbeing of the participants were studied for over 75 years. The results of this extremely long study were fascinating, and crossed any socioeconomic boundaries participants might have. Strong relationships with family and friends was the biggest factor in promoting happiness. Other interesting findings were that reframing and rewriting a negative situation that you have experienced can be a good way of protecting you, helping you maintain a positive outlook on life. Living in the moment, enjoying the now, was also a great way to promote happiness and well-being. Involvement in meaningful, long-term relationships was one of the primary keys to happiness for participants in this study though, and being able to forgive would have been crucial to maintaining these.

It would be brilliant then to educate children so that they understand what forgiveness is and to help them process any negative feelings they have when someone does something wrong to them. It would be useful, too, if they had a method for finding a way of moving forward. So, how could we facilitate this? The following process could be used just after an incident involving an injustice your child has experienced, or you could use previous incidents they have been involved with as examples to use in your discussions. It is useful to draw upon your child's own experiences so that they understand the emotions involved. Real-life scenarios are great for this, such as a friend making an unkind comment, borrowing something without asking or excluding your child from play.

Action

Part 1

Firstly, your child should learn what forgiveness is and also what it isn't. Discussing with your child what forgiveness is would be a great start:

Forgiveness is:

- Your choice to stop the pain you have experienced because of someone else's actions

- Your choice to think about the person who hurt you with kindness, even though you don't have to

- Your choice to let go of any bad feelings you have about what happened. You are entitled to feel them but you choose to let them go.

It is also important to understand what forgiveness is not. It is not:

- Forgetting or excusing the behaviour of the person who hurt you

- Making friends again with the person who hurt you

- Saying that you forgive someone but staying angry inside and wanting revenge.

It is really important that children are heard and their feelings of anger and resentment are accepted as justified in their situation. When they are wronged, they should know that they have the right to be annoyed. Learning how to forgive, however, is necessary so that these feelings don't turn around and hurt them deep inside for a second time.

You can now use your child's situation to begin work on forgiveness. Firstly, help them see what is going on:

1. Ask your child to write down or talk you through what happened.

2. Ask them why the situation was unfair to them. They could tell you their answer or write it down.

3. Try to get them to list all the ways in which they were affected by the situation. This list could include things like they felt angry or sad, they lost something material like a toy or money, it makes them behave differently now like avoiding making new friendships or playing with their favourite toys, perhaps they were physically hurt by the offender or the situation made them change their views on wider things like trusting people or sharing.

Part 2

Now it's time to think about the other person. Ask your child a few things about the person who wronged them:

1. What good things can you list about this person?

2. What bad things could you say about them?

3. What sort of home and school life do you think this person has?

4. Is there anything you think this person might be finding difficult right now?

5. Is there anything that you can think of which might have triggered this person's behaviour?

The person doing the harm might have a difficult home life. They may find school work hard and try to deflect attention away from this by how they behave. They could be jealous in some way of your child, or they may feel insecure themselves and pass this negativity on to make themselves feel better. Their behaviour is not excused by these details, but understanding them may make forgiveness slightly easier to give.

Part 3

Help your child make two lists

- **PROS:** one which lists good things which will happen if they manage to forgive the person who harmed them

- **CONS:** the other which lists bad things which will happen if they forgive the offender.

Make it clear to your child that the person who harmed them has no right to kindness and it's your child's decision alone whether they let go of negative emotions such as anger and resentment and choose to forgive.

In the end, ask your child if their view has changed about the person who hurt them. Has this process changed their mind in any way? It may take some time to come around to forgiveness, so don't push this on them. Allow the process to sink in and come back to it after a period of time. It might take a few days, weeks or even months, but revisit this process each time they experience a problem. When they are ready to forgive, then they can go to the final stage.

Part 4

Going forward…There are several ways to approach forgiveness, depending on whether it feels appropriate to contact the offender or not - contact is not necessary for forgiveness to take place though. Here are some ideas for your child:

1. Cup your hands and, at the same time, think of all the feelings which you experienced after you were wronged. Imagine those feelings are inside you and you can blow them out. Blow them into your cupped hands, then roll them around between your palms and throw them away as far as you can.

2. Write a letter to the person who wronged you. Tell them what they did and how it affected you and that you forgive them. You now have a choice. You can send the letter or simply screw it up into a ball, put it in the bin, tear it up

and throw it away or burn it, getting rid of all those feelings of anger and hurt as you do so.

You may decide to say something to the person who wronged you. A good approach is to tell them that what they did was wrong and it made you feel bad but that you forgive them. Perhaps you could suggest that next time they could do something different. An example of this might be: "I'm angry that you took my pen and lost it. I forgive you - maybe next time, please ask me if you can borrow my things."

Journal Regularly

Background

I've left this until last in the first section of the book as your child may enjoy multitasking with their journaling. Some of the activities I've covered so far would fit very comfortably into a journal. Using journaling to write about things your child is grateful for, recording their goals, or writing down issues they're working through surrounding forgiveness, would work well. Children might even want to write down things in a journal that they've learnt on their journey with strengths or keep a record of the self-affirmations that they've used. Pictures and drawings can also be included in a journal if it helps your child process what's on their mind.

I like to keep the definition of journaling a little bit flexible and leave it up to an individual to take ownership of what they want to record in their journal, as long as thoughts and feelings are part of the mix. Officially, a journal is a place to write about what has happened. Importantly, it should also provide a safe space for the author to discuss their thoughts and feelings about a situation, knowing that it's for their eyes only. This is slightly more than a diary, which may or may not include more personal reflections on events. Due to the very private nature of a journal's content, no one should read a child's journal unless the child grants them permission to do so. For younger children, this may be harder to achieve, but the privacy of older students should be respected. If a child is vulnerable or potentially at risk, then there might be a case for looking at a child's journal without their permission, but if you find yourself in this position, you should probably seek professional help for your child first.

Why bother with writing things in a journal though? How could writing things down possibly make your child happy?

Journaling has many strings to its bow and a decent amount of scientific research shows that it can benefit children, helping them lead happier lives. Historical evidence shows that people have been journaling for centuries - the Roman Emperor Marcus Aurelius left behind a mine of information in his journals, as did Marie Curie and Einstein almost two thousand years later. Interest in the benefits of journaling began in the mid-twentieth century and has grown ever since. In one of the earliest studies, a number of students entering university were divided into two groups. Half were asked to write for 15 minutes for a period of four days on a superficial topic and the other half wrote about a traumatic experience they had had. Over the next six months, the number of times the students who were assigned the journaling task visited the health centre was about half the number of visits the control group made. Writing about their traumatic experiences seemed to enable the students to process the trauma and heal.

Subsequent studies found measurable, physical evidence to support the benefit of writing down your thoughts and feelings - they discovered that participants' immune systems significantly improved. Somehow, the act of writing something difficult onto paper seems to help a person process it and move forward. Incidentally, physical writing has more impact than online journaling, although I have to confess that I do my journaling online.

Other studies have confirmed that journaling, writing down feelings, expressing emotions with words and working through traumas with written language can even have a positive effect on inflammatory or autoimmune conditions such as arthritis or HIV. Many of these studies required participants to journal for a matter of days or weeks, so imagine how powerful this could be if a person got into the habit of journaling at a young age and continued the practice throughout their life.

Journaling can have a very positive effect on stress, anxiety and depression too. In a really interesting study carried out by the University of California, 30 candidates did some matching games using photos of real people with different expressions on their faces. Sometimes they were required to match a label of the emotion, such as 'angry,' to the photo, and in other tests, they matched an angry face with another face with the same expression. There were also matches for gender. We came across the amygdala when looking into mindfulness. When we are in a stressful, potentially dangerous situation, the amygdala comes into action. Sometimes this is absolutely necessary, but the stress response can cause us harm at other times. Incredibly, the study found that simply by labelling an emotion with words, activity in the amygdala was reduced for participants in the study. Essentially, taking emotions and putting them into words measurably reduced the stress response in study subjects.

Much of the research which has been carried out into journaling has been on young people such as university students; studies with younger children on the benefits of journaling have been limited and have largely focussed on children with emotional and behavioural disorders. Interventions with this group have helped reduce emotional outbursts and improved children's emotional control, and some studies have found that participants improved their grades at school. More research is needed with this age group, but I do feel that the evidence is pretty solid that a routine of regular journaling is a great way to allow young minds to process their emotions effectively and therefore be more positive and happy from the inside out.

How, then, can we help our children begin journaling?

Action

Part 1

For younger children who may not be ready to write, help them with the idea of journaling:

1. This is a safe space for you to be creative, to think about and record how you feel.

2. Choose a copybook, notebook or lock-and-key journal and decorate it in any way you like.

3. Find a special place to store it - this is just for you and no one else.

4. Decide on when you are going to add to your journal - as soon as you get home from school, maybe every day just before bed or even on a Friday evening, once a week when you have more time. Whenever you have a difficult experience, be sure to fill out a page in your journal on that day too.

5. When you add to your journal, try to remember anything which happened during the day which made you feel good, bad or unsure. If you have crayons, pens or paints, draw what you feel. You might even do a whole page of red if you're angry, or sunshine with a smile if you had a good experience that day. Cut out, stick in, draw and paint anything which reminds you of how you feel.

Part 2

With older children who can write, steps 1-4 will be the same. Stress that they don't need to worry about spelling, handwriting or grammar. They can just pile their thoughts onto the page as they arrive - it's only for them to read, after all. They might struggle occasionally with where to start and it could be worth using the following questions as writing prompts:

What bothers or annoys you?

What makes you feel happy?

What is the last thing which made you sad?

What ideas have you had recently?

What dreams do you have for your future?

What usually makes you cry?

If you could solve something in this world, what would it be?

How do you feel, right here, right now?

If you could fix something in your life, what would it be?

What are you excited about?

U UNDERSTAND DIFFICULT TOPICS

After your child has highlighted and enhanced a useful batch of strengths and begun to include powerful activities such as mindfulness exercises, using self-affirmations and journaling in their lives, they should be feeling happier, more confident and a little more resilient. Things don't always go to plan in life, though; children may find moving home or changing schools a traumatic experience. They might mix with peers at school who have older siblings that expose them to unsuitable content, or they may even suffer the loss of someone close to them. Of course, every child and every situation is different, but in this section, I wanted to give some insight into issues and possible solutions based on academic research into dealing with difficult topics. If you think your child may be in danger or have concerns about their mental health, please contact a professional for help – this section is more about prevention than cure.

I certainly believe that if parents and children are armed with information and understanding of a topic, then this will afford them some level of protection when problems arise and they will be in a much better position to make good decisions going forward through troubled times.

Drugs, Smoking, and Alcohol

Background

It's probably safe to say that most parents would prefer their children to avoid experimenting with drugs, smoking, and drinking alcohol. Unfortunately, we can't always be by our child's side to help them avoid conversations about these topics with their peers. Children are naturally curious and want to learn more about the world around them. If a subject is deemed 'inappropriate for your age', then you can almost guarantee that they will want to know more and might even try it for themselves if they see others doing it. A member of my family is in the police force and I'm often told I'm not allowed to know any more details about an incident I've read about in the news in which they were involved. The information might well be very boring, but the fact that it's a secret I'm not allowed to be told drives me insane with curiosity. Children are just the same and their journey of discovery in this world is only just beginning so they have a lot to find out.

Much research has identified parent-child connectedness (PCC) and frequent, open, easy communication as having a protective effect on children when it comes to steering them away from the harms of addiction and substance abuse involving drugs, cigarettes and alcohol. Feelings of love, closeness, warmth, and satisfaction lie at the heart of this connection between parent and child, and open communication allows children to feel confident talking to a parent about difficult issues and their associated feelings. When PCC is ineffective and discussions involve negative comments from parents who criticise or use sarcasm, researchers have found that children exhibit measurably higher levels of cortisol in their bodies, indicative of stress, and they are more inclined to ignore advice given by their parents. Less connection between parent and child can also lead young people to see smoking, drinking alcohol and taking drugs as a justified, rebellious act.

The good news is that the reverse is true. More than one study has shown that good PCC and 50-50 communication makes children feel they don't want to disappoint their parents and they take on board the advice they are given. Suppose a parent themselves smokes, drinks heavily or takes drugs. In that case, the greatest PCC and open communication will not be effective in dissuading children from using the substances they see their parents use. Children learn from those around them and leading by example is also necessary here.

The way parents approach conversations about different substances is important too, and an effective strategy is to hold balanced, constructive, two-way conversations rather than lecturing them, as this can have a negative impact on them. The health and legal implications of using alcohol, drugs and cigarettes differ. When it comes to alcohol, reasonable negotiation about the amount your young adult should drink in terms of making sure they stay safe and healthy at the same time works much better than trying to ban them from drinking since it is a legally allowed consumable that has been deemed to be ok for people in appropriate quantities. Your children choosing to take drugs or smoke differs from their drinking alcohol, as the ideal position is that they simply don't do these things. The temptation for parents is to tell their children that smoking and drugs are off-limits and an absolute no-no. This doesn't work. What studies show is effective with these is a balanced, educational, informative discussion of the health risks and consequences of putting these substances in our bodies. I was unaware of these studies when my children were growing up, but almost by accident, this happened to be the approach I took with them when discussing these issues. So far in their lives, they have drunk a minimum amount of alcohol, have never taken drugs and have never smoked. I used this approach because I was entirely motivated by making sure they were safe at all times, so I centred my discussions with them around the health and situational consequences of drug and alcohol use. With smoking, I also talked to them about the historical manipulation by the tobacco industry to make money from people's addiction, despite the obvious health risks; this really hit the mark with my two. Children feel threatened when parents limit discussions to dictating rules and regulations and studies confirm that, unfortunately, they are then more likely to use substances themselves.

One final finding to mention here is peer pressure. In a study carried out by the University of California, researchers found that although parental communication significantly influenced the likelihood of a child using substances, the habits of a child's peers also played a pivotal role in determining whether the children turned to smoking, alcohol, or drug use. As parents, therefore, we have an additional role to play: influencing our child's peer associations.

Action

1. Set an example. This is going to be a really tough one for some people, I know. Try to limit your child's exposure to any substance use and seek professional help if you can't manage this alone.

2. Do your homework. There are plenty of articles online which go through the health risks of smoking, alcohol and the ever expanding range of drugs spilling onto our streets at any given moment. Keep an ear to the ground in your local area and find out what the latest trends are.

3. Open up positive communication and develop great PCC with your child. Gentle, age appropriate discussions about substance use can begin from school age upwards. Opportunities may arise randomly if you see someone inebriated in public, in a movie or have a family member suffering the consequences of a lifetime of smoking, for

example. Aside from physical health risks, help your child understand that some substance abuse can affect their mental health and cause permanent damage. The use of alcohol and drugs can also make them lose their focus and awareness and put them in potentially dangerous situations. For teenagers, they should be made aware of some of the dangers of drugs being given to them without their knowledge. In recent years, venues for evening entertainment for young people have attracted unpleasant individuals who target girls with increasingly creative ways to drug them and then abduct them. Years ago, my daughter's drink was 'spiked', but luckily, she was with a friend when she became incoherent - nowadays, criminals use far more sophisticated methods on victims, so it's worth discussing with your child ways they could make sure they are safe at all times.

4. Keep an eye on your child's friendships. The habits, behaviours and values of peers influence your child. Keep your child's friends close and notice what they are interested in and do. Try to encourage friendships with peers whose families have similar values to your own, alongside working on PCC and developing good communication between yourself and your child.

Sex Education

Background

Our role as parents is to guide, educate and prepare our children for adulthood. Why then, is the subject of sex such a taboo for many of us? For some of you reading this, you will be wondering what I'm on about, but I suspect that for the majority of parents, the idea that we might want to be involved in the process of educating our children about sexual practices and sexual health is pretty daunting.

The question is, would you prefer your child to learn about sex from someone like yourself who has experience of life and has their best interests at heart, or from another child in school who may have gained access to a porn site full of potentially violent, graphic material? Unfortunately, with advancements in technology, access to such material is getting easier and there will always be children who somehow find their way around parental controls. Sex education is also offered in schools, but this often takes place after puberty for some pupils, which is arguably too late and can be an awkward, embarrassing experience for many.

In my experience, hiding information from children makes it appear that the information is in some way shameful, embarrassing or just wrong. If our children do not know about or feel confident discussing what makes a healthy or an unhealthy relationship, it leaves them vulnerable to manipulation by other, more savvy parties. The results of this can be devastating. In a study I read as part of my own research for this book regarding the benefits of journal writing, some of the study participants, a group of students, were asked a side question about whether they had ever experienced a traumatic sexual experience before the age of 17. 15% of the group said they had. These students reported visiting the doctor more often than the other participants and they also suffered more depression and anxiety overall. Interestingly, something which seemed to exacerbate negative symptoms was if they kept the traumatic incident secret. Why would they do this? The answer is usually something to do with shame, embarrassment, or guilt. Attitudes in our society are slowly changing, as it is clearly wrong for a victim of sexual assault to have these feelings, but combatting this should begin at home. As parents, we have the power to arm our children with the correct information and help them foster a positive attitude towards their own bodies and we should provide a non-judgemental place where they can share their trauma should they experience any problems.

The subject of sex is often avoided by parents, deflecting questions on the topic to a discussion about storks, birds and bees. Of course, children find it embarrassing when they finally discover that their own parents actively participate in sexual acts together - they themselves are evidence of this - since their parents have taught them that this is the appropriate reaction.

A review of the last three decades of research in this area shows that when parents play an active role in sex education, this has a protective effect on their children and the result is that their children exhibit less risky sexual behaviours in adolescence. This protective effect has been found to be stronger for girls and also when mothers lead educational discussions. In a study carried out in Iran looking at parent-son communication about sexuality, where adherence to both traditional and religious practices is important to many families in the confusion of a rapidly changing world, researchers noted that a commonly held belief amongst parents was that by talking to children about sex, you encourage them to participate in sexual acts at a younger age. Studies show that the reverse is true. In this study, the researchers concluded that parent-son communication and education about sexuality actually reduced early sexual behaviours. When you explain to your child the physical process of reproduction and discuss important issues relating to sex, such as feelings, values and relationships, your family's values will shine through. In the case of the Iranian families in the study, their preference was for abstinence before marriage, and educating their sons meant that they were more likely to adhere to their family's values. We all have a slightly different take on what makes the perfect relationship and at what age people should become sexually active, so it follows that parents' approaches will vary. What is important is that those discussions do take place and that children get their information from people who care about them and have their best interests at heart.

I know that many parents feel very strongly about how their children should be taught about sex in schools and would like their children to understand their own personal values with regard to relationships and sex. There's a very simple answer to this - make sure you talk to them openly at home and work through your values and ideals with them one to one. Children are curious about the world and want to learn, so give them the information and answer their questions. If you are uncomfortable with your child participating in a sex education programme at school, you are entirely within your rights to request their withdrawal from the programme. However, do ensure that you have already educated them at home, so they are prepared for discussions with their peers at school. Protesting outside the school gates about the content of the programme serves little purpose - it's your responsibility as a parent to educate and protect your children in matters of their health and well-being, so take that step forward and proceed. We teach them how to wash themselves, toilet train them, educate them about which foods are healthy to eat and more, so it's natural that we should teach them about the changes they will undertake at puberty and the reasons why our bodies change.

Action

1. Start young. In my tutoring currently, I don't generally touch upon the subject of sex education, but I have fond memories of a lovely student I taught for a number of years who had incredible parents. I began teaching her when she was age 7 and we ended up having some extremely interesting, thoughtful conversations as she was a wonderfully curious student. One time, when she was only 8 and unprompted by me, she explained how human reproduction worked, all in a matter-of-fact way. She didn't regard sex as shameful, embarrassing or taboo, just something people should know and be open about. Her Mum protected her by educating her on many difficult topics and she grew into a supremely confident young adult, armed with the facts and thus able to make informed decisions about her actions. Everyone is different, but personally, I think that the younger you have gentle, matter-of-fact conversations with children about how humans reproduce, the easier it is. Keeping things hidden and secret makes them appear shameful or wrong in some way, so the sooner the conversation is started, the better. Start off with straightforward, age-appropriate, biological discussions. They should know that intimate parts of their body are their own and other people do not have a right to touch them there without their permission. Over time,

explain that loving relationships should be at the heart of any intimacy.

2. More advice needed. Children will become increasingly curious as they approach High School age and it's important to gradually and sensitively add more complex topics into discussions. Hopefully, by now, they feel comfortable coming to you for answers, so they may well take the lead by asking questions. Non-judgemental, factual answers in the context of your family's values are needed here to keep communication open and maintain trust.

3. It's never too late. If you haven't already talked to your child about sex, you are not alone and it's never too late to make a difference to them. The older they are, the harder it might be. It can feel really awkward and embarrassing for parents but studies have shown that children do appreciate and benefit from communication with their parents on this topic and surely, it's far better they hear it from you than gaining snippets of quite possibly poor advice from their peers or searching for answers online.

Online Safety

Background

I really wanted to find a magic bullet for this one - to be able to say, "Do this, do that and do the other and everything will be fine." In many aspects of life, it ultimately boils down to hard work, thoughtful consideration, progress monitoring, and vigilance. Something we need to acknowledge is that ensuring our children's safety in today's online environment is our responsibility as parents and carers. Technology changes at such a pace that we must stay abreast of new developments in order to protect our children. We cannot depend on security software or the ethics of large corporations to do this for us, and legislative changes are often too slow to take effect given the rapid evolution of the tech industry. The good news is that our intervention as parents does make a huge difference and there are many positive things we can do to help our children get the most out of the online environment and avoid much of its darker side.

Kids will be kids; they have a desire to learn about their world, and the edgier the content, the more intriguing it becomes. They also want to fit in, so it is natural for them to want to be part of the group and join in the banter on social media as soon as they can get away with it. These desires potentially open them up to a world filled with images they will find disturbing and abuse from people they both know and have never met. We might be tempted to keep them away from smartphones, ban then from using the internet and immediately disable all devices in our homes. The way the world works this century, there's almost nowhere to hide from the online space. Just like water, it will find a path to trickle through and, just like water, it is necessary for your children to be able to access it in order for them to function in society as adults. There are many benefits to children of accessing technology of course; it has opened up new methods to learn, helped young people to communicate with their peers and families more readily and provides access to a seemingly limitless supply of quality information, knowledge and resources for enquiring minds. Almost the exact reverse of these are true - our children are also exposed to dangerous material that could harm them and be subject to malicious social interactions. It's worth taking a deeper look at what is going on.

A longitudinal study was published in 2023, which looked at the impact of a child acquiring a mobile phone and if it made a difference at which age they had access to it. Children's grades, sleep and mental health were assessed on an annual basis and over 250 children took part in the study over a five-year period; surprisingly, the results showed that after children had been given a smartphone of their own, there was no significant increase in their rates of depression, children with a mobile phone actually slept slightly longer than those without, and there was no correlation between them having a phone and their grades changing either up or down in school. Also, it didn't make any difference which age children were given the smartphone. When a study shows no result, this can in itself be significant, as it is here. Other studies have pointed to some level of sleep issues and grade reduction for younger children having their own smartphones, but the results vary. Having the online environment freely available in your pocket is an incredible gift and it would appear that access to this resource is not the cause of problems, so let's dig a little deeper still and look at social media.

Humans are social animals, and our connections with other people are vital for our happiness and mental health. When children use social media platforms simply to communicate with close friends and family, this is a significant positive. However, peer pressure and the desire to fit in can push children to strive for popularity, surrounded by a multitude of adoring 'friends' who admire their pictures and posts on their social media profiles. They connect with a wider range of people - less 'friends', more 'acquaintances' - and this is where problems may begin. What happens when someone doesn't have many so called 'friends' following them or when their posts receive little attention in the form of 'likes'? Our body's reaction to 'likes' is the same as when we play a slot machine - the pleasure process gives us a wonderful dose of dopamine, leaving us wanting more. This is a slippery slope towards addiction. Adults find this hard to resist and for children, who haven't yet exercised and developed the area of their brain responsible for self-control, it's even worse. It is reported that one of the founders of the Facebook 'Like' button, Justin Rosenstein, has actually deleted the Facebook app on his own devices as he finds social media such a toxic environment. When your children only connect with genuine, close friends, it's good, but when the net is widened, they could open themselves up to comments from people who don't truly care about them personally and they may feel deflated by the response to their posts.

When young people repeatedly see images of their peers and idols online looking their best (quite possibly having used enhancement tools to improve the photos before they are posted), this can have a negative effect on children's feelings about their own bodies. An interesting thing to note is that one study carried out on high school students showed that students who posted more pictures of themselves were more dissatisfied with their own bodies than those who posted less. Perhaps, in some strange way, people post pictures to convince themselves that they look good because they are insecure inside. Rather than being intimidated by all the great-looking people in the photos, maybe we should feel compassion for them instead.

Many other studies have certainly confirmed that the use of social media negatively impacts children's body image. Actual body images of our children need to be considered too. Children require protection from manipulative peers, groomers and potential paedophiles who may ask them to share photos of intimate body parts online. Children need to understand that they don't always see the true picture of what is going on in social media feeds and they need to be confident about what to say when asked to participate in harmful photo sharing.

With regards to inappropriate material, there is, of course, a whole world of material out there we would not want our children to view, some of which I cover in the sections on sex education, drugs, smoking and alcohol. There are measures we can put in place to limit this on our children's devices and in our network at home, but their peers may still have access and your child ends up exposed to it anyway. For this reason, I suggest the steps below to limit access whilst at the same time educating your child so that they can become part of their own protection unit, alongside you.

Action

1. Educate yourself. The most important thing you can do as a parent is keep up with technology yourself. Social media platforms and online sites rise, fall, come and go. You need to be aware of what's going on. Look on apps and sites so that you understand how they work and what they contain, and only then can you make informed decisions about what your child should have access to. If you have a strong, trusting relationship with your child, perhaps

check these things out together. Forums on sites like Mumsnet and Netmums can help too.

2. Be careful what you post. Getting your child's first photo from an ultrasound scan is such an exciting moment, and it's understandable that you want to share this with the world. From the moment you post it on a social media platform however, you are also inviting strangers to advertise their products to you and your child is front and centre stage. Really, you should ask your child their permission to have their pictures posted online, but in reality, this would be silly. What you do need to do is make thoughtful decisions about what pictures of them you post yourself. You never know who might be watching.

3. Follow age ratings. Most games have a recommended age rating and social media platforms are only suitable for ages 13 and above. Children do try to gain access to games and platforms below recommended ages and it's up to you as a parent to notice when this happens. When your child gets their first smartphone, tablet or computer, the deal is that you have access to it and will regularly keep an eye on the apps and sites they use it for. This is for their own protection because you love them, want them to enjoy using the phone and want the best for them. You may need to have your wits about you as children are very smart, especially with new trends, and often find ways around the

rules by, for example, creating separate accounts for their families and peers.

4. Explain the dangers to your child. Tell them that you only have their best interests at heart and want to keep them safe, not spoil any fun. You cannot protect them fully, so they need to take on board some responsibility themselves. Having this trusting, open relationship with your child is their biggest protection. Even if you can't quite believe it now, they look up to you and do listen carefully to your advice when it is clearly given for their own good. Arm your children with the information so they can protect themselves alongside you. Explain, for example, that if someone asks your child to send pictures of intimate parts of their body to them, this is wrong. Talk through what can happen if they are manipulated into doing this and explain how devastating the consequences can be. The person doing this might be someone they physically have contact with, but children can also be manipulated into sharing inappropriate pictures by people with power, success and internet 'fame'. Groomers like these have been operating in one form or another for many years, using the technology of the era to manipulate young people. Many of Jimmy Saville's victims were vulnerable young girls who did not have the protection, guidance and support of parents - a reason, I'm sure, they were

targeted. Talk to your child about apps that seem free but, in the small print, are collecting personal information about your children from their phones all the time. Explain that sites with dodgy content can send viruses to their devices. Talk about body image - reassure your child that images can be manipulated easily and people generally only post pictures that make them seem like they're having an amazing time, often hiding a rather less enjoyable reality. It is not possible to have hundreds of close friends, so explain to your child that there is no need for them to feel bad if they have fewer followers than other people; the quality of interaction with close friends is far more important. If people online are having such a great social life, why do they have so much time to spend on social media? Pictures posted do not equal reality. If your child receives unpleasant messages from someone in school, take a screenshot, go into school and report the incident. Schools are now taking these things seriously and should act. If someone outside their physical circle of friends begins messaging your child, advise them to be cautious, particularly if the other person suggests they keep their friendship secret. The profile picture might appear to be of a child, but it may not be. If they express a desire to meet, ensure your child arranges this through you. If your child wishes to tag their location on social media, advise them to do so only after they have moved to a new location. These are just a few talking points about how to stay safe online, and I'm certain there are many more. The most crucial factor is to engage in conversation, providing your child with the necessary information so that you can work together as a team for their protection, while simultaneously enjoying all the wonderful benefits of the online space.

5. Teach your child to be kind online. I've talked a lot here about what other people share online but it's also worth having a conversation about what your child might decide to share online. They may well not realise that what they post stays there forever. Some organisations routinely inspect candidates' profiles when recruiting so, from the moment children begin their online journey, they need to be aware of the effect their online footprint may have in their futures. If they would be uncomfortable saying something in person to someone, then this is definitely something they should not say online. A good rule to go by is always be kind in your comments and if you have nothing good to say, then don't say anything at all.

6. Step up security. Investigate the parental controls on all your child's devices. Google provides a tool for limiting content, but there are also child-friendly search engines available. Depending on the device, it might be appropriate to install virus-scanning software to hunt

down malware or spyware which might come from infected sites such as movie or music-sharing platforms. Double-check your child's devices for software updates on a regular basis too, and change their passwords frequently for additional security.

7. Educate your children about scams. Online scams are becoming increasingly well-planned and difficult to spot. Children need to be kept up to date with these, particularly if any of their devices are connected to payment details. Settings on their email should filter out scams and they should know not to click on any link via an email, even if it seems legitimate. If they are not sure, they should ask you.

8. Monitor screen time. Most parents I work with currently have set up time limits for their children's devices. I've seen firsthand the addictive element of online games, social media platforms and YouTube channels and it's important for children to follow other interests in their spare time. It's good to use the technology available, but it's also great to exercise some of those other skills important for your child's development.

9. Keep devices out of the bedrooms at bedtime. Blue light emitted by devices and the temptation to have yet another

last look at our screens makes the value of this last action an easy one to appreciate.

Bullying

Background

Definitions of bullying vary, but in essence, bullying is behaviour by one person who hurts another person, either physically or emotionally, and which repeatedly happens over a period of time. Bullying is usually accompanied by an imbalance of power between children and is intentional. It's a systematic abuse of power. Groups of individuals may be involved as either perpetrators or victims. For a snapshot of the extent to which bullying is happening, in the UK ONS Crime Survey for 2017-2018, 22% of 10-year-olds said that they had been bullied. In the US, the National Centre for Educational Statistics reported similar findings for the same year amongst all students - that's more than 1 in 5 of our children experiencing bullying on a regular basis. Other surveys have found that 1 in 3 of all children have experienced bullying at some point in their childhood. What used to be limited to the playground or the walk home from school, bullying now occurs in increasingly diverse and intrusive locations and it's a challenge for parents, educational establishments and any form of legislation to keep up. With the online environment continuing to grow, the nature of and opportunities for bullying continue to expand.

It's useful to understand where bullying might stem from in evolutionary terms. Bullying makes more sense if we go back to primeval times, when individuals had to fight for status, access to resources, dominance and mating rights. Bullies want to control and improve their own position by hurting other people with lower perceived status than themselves. Bullying isn't just a minor irritation or rite of passage, as some people seem to think; the behaviour of bullies can have physical effects on both themselves and their victims. Scientists are able to measure levels of a particular protein in our blood, the C-reactive protein (CRP), which can be an indicator of how likely someone is to suffer from metabolic disorders, cardiovascular disease and mental health issues in their lives. In one study, when blood samples were taken from victims of bullying, their blood contained raised levels of CRP. When these same victims were tested again between the ages of 19 and 21, after the bullying had stopped, CRP levels remained raised. Interestingly, CRP levels in their bullies were lower even than CRP levels in children who were neither bullies nor victims. On re-testing at ages 19-21, the levels of CRP for bullies was about half that of their victims. Putting it in a nutshell, bullying improves the well-being of bullies at the expense of their victim's own health.

I've only discussed one particular type of bully. We find this type of person in a wide variety of societies and cultures today; they are often popular, have good social skills, are manipulative, callous, lack empathy, and are intent on being dominant. They come from all socioeconomic backgrounds, including wealthy families, and can be successful in their adult lives. There is another sort of individual, however, who also exhibits bullying behaviour - those who have experienced being a victim themselves and subsequently behave like a bully. This sort of child is often not as popular as the individuals discussed above. They have less well-developed social skills and often come from lower socioeconomic backgrounds. The outcome for these individuals is frequently poor in adulthood in terms of health and economic prospects. Personally, I have more sympathy for these individuals, but at the end of it all, they are still trying to benefit themselves by hurting other people with their actions.

Levels of a particular protein in someone's blood are one thing, but there are many more consequences of bullying, which are well documented in research papers - sleep problems, depression, anxiety, poorer academic achievement, lower income prospects as an adult and victims are even more likely to catch a cold. With such high percentages of children reporting having been bullied, why aren't our governments taking this more seriously as, surely, our countries are taking a hit from this in terms of productivity when victims of bullying move into adulthood?

Bullies might benefit from their actions on an individual level, but society as a whole suffers. There's a reduction in the productivity of adults who have been the victims of bullying, and working together, listening to colleagues and showing understanding and empathy is how great things are achieved. Breakthroughs in technology, science and medicine have only happened via communication, cooperation and teamwork. Countries whose citizens score the highest in terms of happiness, like the Nordic countries, have more equal societies with generous social security and healthcare packages – I don't think the generosity, equality and compassion shown in these countries are very high on a bully's list of priorities. At the other end of the happiness scale come the countries run by dictatorships - states ruled by dominance, instability and bullying tactics.

Unfortunately, bullying is not easy to stop or help our children avoid, but there are things we can do as parents. Most of the activities outlined in the first section of this book will make your child more resilient, happy and full of confidence and self-worth. Their social skills and therefore their ability to make and keep friends will have been enhanced too. These are things that keep bullies away. Parents have only a limited reach and, as always, it's important to keep an open dialogue with your child so that you can help them identify bullying if it happens. You want them to feel comfortable coming to you to talk it through; plus, you can talk through tactics to protect them too.

Action

Part 1

Keep an open dialogue. The most important thing to do is talk to your child about relationships with other children and help them understand what is and isn't acceptable. If they can express their thoughts with you freely and know that you will always react without judgement, this protects them. If they do experience bullying, it can sometimes be useful to use role play to help them feel comfortable deflecting any approach from the bully the next time it happens. In this Action section are suggestions on approaches to take; a couple of them will hopefully make the bully stop and think, but I also think it's important that your child realises that they are the one in control of how they react to any given situation and they can actually choose to reduce how much they are hurt by someone else emotionally. If the bullying is physical, then this will also, of course, have an emotional impact.

Your child can only influence someone else, not change them. They do, however, have the ability to change their own reactions to what has happened. In any situation involving someone else who bullies or hurts them in some way, your child has a choice. Certainly, the other party has done something wrong, but your child may not necessarily be able to change them or their actions, or what they might do next. Your child can cry, stay in bed for days, mope around feeling hurt, become depressed, wonder why the bully didn't even notice their reaction, and overall, make themselves feel much worse. This compounds the hurt and, on top of that, they were the victim in all of this in the first place, making it doubly unfair. Meanwhile, the bully who hurt them initially, quite often, simply doesn't care.

It would be great if your child could cut out the extra hurt they received and even limit the emotional turmoil the bullying created. If your child is feeling secure and focused on his or her own strengths and knows their own self-worth, then the first line of defence, when bullied, is to fall back on this resilience and refuse to take offence. As Eleanor Roosevelt put it, "No one can make you feel inferior without your consent." Encourage your child to ask the questions, Who did wrong in this situation? - Whose fault is it? - Does anyone deserve to be treated like this? - Would you treat someone else like this?. Why should they feel at all bad that someone else has done something wrong? The other person has the problem, not them. They have nothing to feel bad about inside themselves.

It can help to employ the strength of perspective with this, particularly if the bully is someone who has been a victim of bullying themselves. Bullies crave power and attention and are desperately trying to fulfil a need within themselves by behaving as they do. A study published in 2016 looked at bullying-type behaviour in mice. It was found that there is a part of the brain which, for some mice, rewards aggressive, dominant behaviour rather than subdues it. This is relatively new research, but we may well discover that people who tend to bully have a psychiatric disorder which could be treated in the future. Talking this through with your child can help them find some degree of compassion and forgiveness which might help your child feel better inside. This is not condoning the abuse, but finding a way of letting it go.

Part 2

Ignore the bully. I was not bullied in school and this was my method of avoiding their gaze. What a bully really wants is to enjoy seeing a reaction in their target. No reaction = no reward. People occasionally said horrible things to me but I would just pretend I didn't hear them - which is weird because I obviously had heard them - and I might move away or start a conversation with another person. It certainly worked for me. You're saying that what they have said means nothing to you and is of no importance, the ultimate put-down for someone desperate for attention. Online, don't respond; block the other person. Remember, they are desperate for that reward, so don't give it to them.

Part 3

Respond, but not in the way they want. For this to work, keep cool, act bored, unfazed and disinterested so that the bully doesn't get their reward. They will soon learn that you will not give them what they want. Only respond in a neutral, unflustered way; otherwise, just ignore them or walk away.

"So?"

"If I'm such a freak and you're the one following me around, what does that say about you?"

"And why exactly is my hairstyle of interest to you?"

"Is there nothing more interesting in your life than my shoes?"

"And I should care, why?"

Part 4

Call them out. This must only be done if your child feels confident doing so and won't come across as being hurt and destroyed, which again, will give the bully a reward. Sometimes it is good for bullies to be told that what they are doing is wrong though, getting called out for their actions. It must be done in an uncluttered, neutral, matter-of-fact way though; otherwise, it is best to avoid responding.

"Does saying that make you feel good?"

"What you're doing is wrong."

"That's a mean thing for someone to say."

"This is what a bully would say or do."

Encourage positive friendships. Bullies find it much easier to harass someone who is isolated and alone than anyone in a crowd since they usually have increased confidence to respond in this way. If your child is new to a school, arrange play dates and try to encourage them to form new friendships as soon as possible in order for them to grow a protective layer of people around them.

6. Give your child the experience of alternative social settings. Involving your child in activities and clubs in different social contexts puts them in other environments and helps them to see that they can in fact interact with other people perfectly well, even if they are experiencing problems in school. Suppose you choose an activity which your child excels at or has a particular interest in. In that case, they will learn that they can in fact be a valued member of society, which will go a long way to mending any damage caused by bullying elsewhere.

7. Escalate if appropriate. If your child is bullied in school and they have tried deflection techniques with no success, inform the school. This is where an open dialogue with your child will help, as they will probably feel that intervention might make things worse for them in school. Explain your concern to the staff involved. If the bullying is affecting their sleep, health, mental health, or happiness, then it needs to be stopped. Collect evidence by making a note of when and where the bullying has occurred and ensure your child takes screenshots of anything happening

online. Go to their class teacher first. If there isn't sufficient response or a resolution, then take it to the next professional further up the chain of command in your child's school. Be an annoying parent and push for your child to get justice - when the research is out there telling us that bullying can both physically and emotionally harm our children for life, it's simply not good enough for schools to ignore us. If there has been any violence or threats to your child's life, take your evidence straight to the police.

Difficult Truths

Background

Life is definitely not always straightforward. Moving home, changing schools, relationship problems and death cross all our paths at some point and each time, hopefully, we get through it and our resilience increases ever so slightly because we learn that we have the ability to survive trying times. Children have little experience to draw upon, so any of these problems can seem scary, confusing and insurmountable, and, as parents, we must tread carefully. Whatever life throws at our families, we should keep talking with our children - go there, be honest and not brush things under the carpet. Children appreciate being told the truth in simple terms and at an appropriate level for their understanding. Children also like routines and normality, so it's important to try to keep these going despite any situation you are going through.

When things get tough, children also need to know you are their rock and that they are loved and appreciated.

In this section, I include a discussion on a number of topics that can impact children's happiness and mental health. There are plenty of other important situations that I could have included, but much of the advice on how to approach helping your child can be adapted. No two situations will be the same, so a degree of flexibility is always needed. As a parent, you know your child better than anyone else and will be the best judge of what level to pitch discussions with your child.

Action

Part 1

Moving house or school. A fairly comprehensive, longitudinal study was carried out involving nearly 20000 US children, regularly assessing their social and behavioural development plus academic skills from kindergarten to eighth grade. The study focussed specifically on the impact on children of house moves during this period in childhood. Researchers considered whether any effects were more or less depending on the child's age when they moved house and whether a change to the child's school made a difference too. Results showed that house moves had a negative effect on children's social and emotional well-being and academic performance, plus there was a tendency towards them developing behavioural issues following the change. The effect might be small with one move, but each additional house move multiplies these negative effects for the children involved. The other interesting finding was that children who moved when in early or middle childhood felt the impact of a house move more than middle to adolescent children, and the negative effects lasted years. Older children also suffered but the effects lasted for a shorter period of time. Understandably, it was found that moving schools as well as houses increased the negative effect on children's academic performance and cognitive skills.

Children love routines and a house move necessitates upheavals in routines. Unfortunately, with increased instability on a world scale in our employment and housing markets, some parents simply have no choice but to move family homes. If you are a parent who is thinking of moving house, try to hold off making that move until your children are a little older. This is sometimes not possible of course, so it would be good to explore ways to minimise potential negative consequences.

- Try to arrange it so that your child's things are the last to be packed and the first to be unpacked. If possible, send them off to school from one home and bring them home to the new home. Perhaps even treat them to a couple of days with grandparents or a family friend they are used to staying with until their room is ready and set up how they are used to it.

- Before moving, check out any timings for school routes and, if you will need to wake up a bit earlier to be on time, begin rising at this time whilst in your old house before the move happens.

- If they are in school, speak to their teachers about the changes that will happen so that they are aware of this and know the dates when changes will be taking place. The school will be more understanding and able to help should your child behave in any way out of character or be tired or less focussed in class.

- Continue to give your child your time and care as usual, even though it's such a busy time for you. Remember that adults fare much better than children under pressure, so just being there like you normally are will go a long way to reassuring them that everything is going to settle down and be fine. As a priority, give them space to carry out their normal play, homework and activities, plus stick to the same eating and sleeping routines. This will soften the blow for them and dampen down any negative effects they might experience.

Part 2

Relationship problems. Family dynamics have changed dramatically in the last century, especially in the West. The norm used to be for children to be raised by both of their married biological parents, but the percentage of children in this category has reduced. In 2022, for example, the figure stood at around 76% in the US. Single parents and same-sex couples make up a large proportion of the remaining 24%. Change can be a good thing, though. Having a society that allows a parent to leave a violent or abusive relationship is important for both parent and child. I am thankful that the cruelty and shame inflicted on unmarried mothers and their children in the past has been recognised for its inhumanity. Same-sex marriages seem to be beneficial for children too. In a longitudinal study carried out in the first country to legalise same-sex marriage, the Netherlands, nearly 3000 children - mostly with married, lesbian parents - were monitored from birth. Their progress through school was compared with over 1000000 children with male and female parents. Children raised from birth by same-sex parents outperformed children raised from birth by mixed-sex parents all the way through school - in both primary and secondary education.

These are the good news stories, but as we all know, life throws all sorts of things at us, so what strategies might we employ to protect our children when relationships don't quite go according to plan? When parents or partners struggle to get on, this can hurt any children they care for. I've used the word 'can' here on purpose since the majority of children whose parents go through a divorce come through just fine - they do not suffer exceptional behavioural issues, lowered school grades or emotional problems.

A higher proportion of children whose parents have split up, however, do suffer from these issues. The question is, what is the difference between the children who sail through a family breakup and those who suffer?

With divorce or separation, children suffer the loss of a parent, they can be affected financially, they can be left with a distracted carer, they might witness conflict between parents, they might need to move house or school and they may witness their carer's internal struggles with the situation. In studies, it has been shown that some of these factors are significant and others not so, and this gives us clues as to how best to protect our children in any relationship turmoil.

1. Arguing, fighting, violence and conflict all affect children badly. If this can't be helped then it might be time to consider removing yourself or your child from the situation. Try really hard not to fight with your partner in front of your child, or at all. Relationship mediators may be able to help, and it's also worth remembering that all parties in a break-up usually want to maintain contact with their children, so it's in everyone's long-term interests to keep it civil. Arguments about and during children's visits also cause harm. Additionally, if a child is going to live with one parent and the other parent is going to move out, in order for your child to avoid suffering loss, make sure

they maintain contact with the absent parent so that it feels like a change rather than a bereavement.

2. After a break up, if the remaining parent has trouble adjusting to the situation, children can be badly affected. We may feel angry, resentful or simply sad, but we should not pass this on to our children. Life sucks sometimes but, as parents, we've got to suck it up ourselves for the sake of our children. They look to us for leadership, strength and love, especially when big changes occur in their lives. Look to the future with positivity, find things to be grateful for and reach out to other adults for some emotional support rather than your own children.

3. Carry on being a great parent. Most parents manage to continue as normal following relationship upheaval - maintaining routines, monitoring homework, organising play dates, and always listening to and loving their children. If your parenting skills slip, this can affect your children, so notice it and take action.

Keeping your cool with your partner, staying positive and maintaining routines with your child will protect them from any negative consequences of relationship issues.

Part 3

Bereavement. As with all of the topics in this book, children are unique and different and experience things in their own way, so parents will need to take a view on their approach to this based on their own child's situation. I've read research papers on this topic and I include recommendations in this section based on these to help children deal with bereavement.

Multiple studies have shown that the death of a parent lowers children's educational achievement, lowers their optimism about the future and work prospects, lowers their confidence, makes them more likely to end up with psychiatric issues, impairs their ability to form relationships themselves and can even hinder their ability to parent. Similar effects are seen with the death of a sibling and of course, the death of anyone close to a child or a pet will affect them too. This is quite an intimidating list, so what can we possibly do to help children carry on with life with confidence, optimism and hope?

A few factors seem to play a part in affecting outcomes for children who suffer a bereavement - the status of a child's mental health prior to the bereavement, parent-child relationships, family cohesion through the event and the response of remaining carers.

Some studies have had long-term success in mitigating the negative consequences of bereavement by using interventions regularly over several months. For example, tasks for parents included learning to actively listen to their child, going out of their way to have one-to-one time with each of their children, appreciating their children in a positive way by catching them doing something good, setting and achieving goals together to generate hope and optimism and engineering positive family time together.

Overall, when a child suffers the loss of someone close:

1. Children need the person who cares for them to be their rock, holding it together themselves whilst empathising with their child's grief and listening to their concerns.

2. Children need to be guided and taught how to look positively forward beyond their grief at the possibilities out there for them. Creating and achieving goals will help here - take a look at the section on optimism.

3. Children need to feel a cloak of support around them. This is done with communication, family activities and the continuation of routines.

I would also urge you to consider the following, but the first suggestion may not be suitable for all children:

1. For any funeral or burial arrangements, allow your child to take part in some way if they feel they would like to. This could be by reading a poem, choosing a hymn or simply by being there during the ceremony or shortly afterwards. Beforehand, explain the whole process in simple terms to them so that there are no surprises on the day. Answer any of their questions about death in gentle

but straightforward language at an appropriate level for their age.

2. Depending on your child's age, there are some lovely books out there which can help a child process what has happened. If you search online, there are plenty of options and they can really help parents begin a conversation.

3. Spend time making a memory box with your child containing special items which remind them of their loved one. This might include a ring, watch, Mother's Day card, perfume, model airplane their Grandad made, favourite mug and so on. Your child could also write down how they feel towards the person who has died - journaling like this is very powerful.

G GATHER YOUR HAPPINESS

Sometimes, we need a boost of happiness and that's what this section is all about. Previous sections have looked at how to build a resilient base on which happiness can grow and protect it from being taken away but this part is to do with actively pulling happiness into our children's lives.

Our bodies are incredible and can naturally give us a happiness boost via the production of hormones. If your child has been a bit down or stressed and is struggling to shift their mood in a positive direction, then it's time to dive into this collection of happiness tools. These activities are also a great way of keeping your child in a happier place, even when things are going smoothly for them.

There are four hormones associated with happiness which we will tap into in this section: dopamine, serotonin, oxytocin and endorphin.

Dopamine makes us feel great when we achieve goals, win things, complete tasks, eat food and go out of our way to look after ourselves.

Serotonin at normal levels in our bodies makes us feel calm and happy and helps us get a good night's sleep. It is sometimes called a mood regulator. Spending time outside on a sunny day, appreciating nature, exercising and carrying out mindful activities all help our bodies produce just the right levels of this hormone.

Oxytocin makes us feel fantastic when we share a big hug, stroke a beloved pet or play with babies and puppies.

Endorphins are natural pain killers which make us feel euphoric and give us a general sense of well-being. We feel their effects after a heavy workout, when we do a random act of kindness, as we listen to or play music, when we laugh or eat dark chocolate and even when we smell lavender essential oil.

Surprises

When we are surprised by something, whether good or bad, the dopamine system in our brains is activated. Surprises can take on many forms, and I would, of course, suggest that we focus on good surprises rather than bad if we want to create some surprises of our own!

Surprises are an opportunity for us to spread some sunshine and show someone special that we care. As a parent, you could sew the seed of surprise within your family and, you never know, your children might eventually begin planting their own. This has certainly happened in my family. Surprises could be post-it notes with special messages written on them, hidden in carefully selected places - perhaps behind the toothbrush pot to surprise your child in the morning, on the inside of someone's bag or, my favourite, just under the covers of someone's bed so that they find it at bedtime. Drawings, handmade cards, little bags of treats and tiny toys could replace the notes. My daughter really likes ducks and, when she was at university, my son bought 100 mini rubber ducks online and he and I hid them all over her college room whenever we visited her - drawers, handbags, laptop bag, bed, laundry basket etc were stuffed with ducks. It was so much fun and brought a huge smile to my daughter's face, plus it took her ages to work out who was doing it, which made us smile too. My son, who is in his late twenties, is still spreading surprises and told me only last week that he's planning the same duck surprise for his best friend, but this time he's hiding dinosaurs...

Like surprises, special treats can also be planned in advance. If someone in the family has a birthday in the dead of winter, perhaps give them an unbirthday celebration over the summer months. Every member of the family could have an unbirthday six months after their actual date - a mirror birthday. Rather than spending lots of money on gifts, perhaps they get to choose a cake and party food for their celebration and an activity for the occasion. They could even choose a theme for their day and everyone in the family could create their own costume to wear as fancy dress.

Another way of activating your surprise system is to try a new activity every so often. Perhaps arrange for your family to have a go at a golf driving range, take an archery lesson, try an orienteering course or even try meditating with horses (a friend of mine works with horses doing this, which gave me the idea to add it here as an example). A few years ago, I arranged a family trip to an indoor skydiving experience - I wouldn't go again, but it was memorable and made us all laugh - mostly at me, though :)

Nature

Spending time outside exercising or just noticing all the plants, animals and terrain around us naturally boosts levels of serotonin, our body's personal happiness regulator. Children are curious and the natural world is forever changing, providing them with something new and awe-inspiring to discover almost daily. I was lucky enough to spend a great deal of my childhood playing outside, noticing changes in colours as the seasons cycled around, breathing in the warm smells of summer and watching as the myriad of grasses in fields near my home shot up and blossomed before a chill in the air brought me back inside for the winter months. Some children still do spend hours in the fresh air, but many don't. Sometimes it helps to have an activity to do to encourage them to explore the natural environment and thus reap all the benefits that this brings.

Regular outdoor sports groups, dog walks and playing in a park or garden are all great, but why not be a little creative? How about your child planting and growing some seeds of their own? Seeds could be grown in a garden but could also thrive on a balcony or windowsill if you don't have access to one. Wildflower seeds can also be sown directly into the soil outside and can give everyone a beautiful surprise when they come into bloom. Perhaps your child could secretly choose a spot to sow these and wait for the results to spring up, surprising everyone.

It's wonderful to watch things grow. If growing seeds proves difficult, garden centres often sell small tomato and chilli plants in springtime and these can provide an alternative to growing things from seed. Already established plants are slightly easier to achieve success with.

Lying down in a quiet place outside can be a fascinating experience. On their back, your child is in a good position to observe clouds. What shapes can they see forming and collapsing above them in the clouds? If they close their eyes, what sounds can they hear? This activity can be done at night time too, if the sky is clear, to observe passing stars. Your child may wish to use a mat under them for this if it is cold. There is plenty of child-friendly information about constellations online if this sparks their interest. They could even get creative and make a sundial for the garden out of rubbish from the recycling bin.

Tree bark comes in a wide variety of textures and your child might enjoy putting together a set of crayon rubbings from different trees. Research the names of different trees, invest in top trumps for trees or flowers and your child could even learn how to work out the age of a tree.

Birds bring so much energy and excitement to a garden. In the winter months, they can be desperate for food and there are some really easy and fun recipes online for fat balls you could make for your garden to help them out. If you position a bird feeder near a window, your child could watch the birds enjoying the fruits of their labour from indoors, inside the warm.

There's something for everyone in the great outdoors and it's just a question of finding a fascinating niche for your child. On a sunny day, parents can join in, enjoying some happiness regulation inside their bodies as well.

Happy Board

This activity takes a little time and thought to put together and your child will need to decide how they want to present their findings - they will be creating their own Happy Board. A pin board, wipeable board or an A3 sheet of card could be used to record your child's happy collection.

Ask them to think of anything which makes them happy. For example, this could be particular people like Mum and Dad, grandparents and friends. It might be certain special animals, pets, plants or flowers. Perhaps a place they visited made them feel amazing, or somewhere they go regularly makes them feel at peace. They might love the smell of something like baking bread, freshly mown grass or a strongly scented rose. There may be special sounds that make them smile, such as the sound of waves, the sound of an owl hooting or a piece of music. Is there a favourite food that makes them happy or something they like to touch which makes them feel great, such as a special blanket or the bark of a particular tree?

Your child can now use their imagination to record these items on their Happy Board - all the many things that make them smile and increase their happiness. They might use photos, drawings, wrappers, dried flowers, or even learn some calligraphy skills to write out a beautiful list. Life is dynamic, so your child should regularly review their board to see if they want to add anything or move things around - they will make new friends, travel to interesting places and discover more things that make them smile. Their collection is a permanent work in progress.

Whenever they are feeling a bit down, they can review their Board as a reminder of the many things that make them smile. It will give them ideas of things they can do straight away to lighten their load and bring them back to a happier place. Even just planning to do something they enjoy or remembering a good experience can trigger those amazing, happy hormones and make your child feel good.

Happy Box

After your child has collected people, things and experiences that make them happy and brought them together on their Happy Board, it's time to make a physical collection of items to make them smile. Perhaps they could decorate a cardboard box in their favourite colours or maybe you have an old, wooden box in your house that could be transformed into a Happy Box for your child. Including items that your child could cuddle encourages their bodies to produce oxytocin. Laughing at a silly joke might prompt the release of endorphins, and if they were to cook, share and enjoy tasting the perfect recipe, their bodies might reward them with a little dopamine.

Your child can put into their Happy Box anything which makes them happy, smile or laugh out loud. They could always begin with items from their Happy Board. My daughter loves essential oils and I know that at the top of her list would be a small bottle of lavender oil alongside a strongly scented candle. Everyone is so different, but here are a few ideas to get you started: a cuddly blanket, funny board or card games, whoopee cushion, bubble blowing set, silly dressing-up outfits, emergency dark chocolate, handwritten recipe cards of favourite dishes, birthday or Christmas cards from special people, joke books, colourful smiley socks, letters or printed emails which contain a lovely message, a much loved cuddly toy, a favourite book, a craft set, doodling books and so on.

Happy Playlists

When we listen to music or laugh out loud during a film, endorphins are released, helping us feel on top of the world. Similarly, when we listen to soothing sounds, our bodies relax. Technology changes so rapidly that I can only recommend your child create their own playlists of Happy Music, Happy Films, and Happy Sounds, but the platform they access these on will depend on the technology of the time and what you have available in your circumstances.

Are there any songs that make your child smile, dance or bounce around? Were they in a certain setting having an amazing time when a particular song was playing? Songs can invoke incredibly powerful memories and take us right back to emotions we have experienced. With your child, try to put together a Happy Music playlist of a few songs with a special meaning for them - perhaps the words are super joyful, or the rhythm just makes them want to dance or the whole song reminds them of a brilliant time.

The sound of rain fills me with horror, as I have lived in a property prone to flooding, but my daughter has always absolutely loved going to sleep to this sound - I know she still uses it to drift off to sleep, even as an adult. There are some great tracks out there that bring sounds of nature into our homes. For example, if your child likes the sound of waves, thunderstorms, crackling fires, cats purring or even the busy murmurings of the Amazon rainforest, then these would be great additions to their Happy Sounds playlist.

Can you think of any movies that made your child laugh out loud? These would be the perfect ones to include in their Happy Movies playlist. I love comedies, so for me, this playlist is pretty long and forever changing.

When your child is feeling a little blue and in need of a pick me up, reach for the playlists, sit back and enjoy a blast of happiness.

Kindness and Charity

When we are kind and helpful to others, oxytocin and endorphins are released in our bodies. Showing kindness doesn't have to be a big affair; it can be as small as holding the door open for a busy teacher. Lending a pencil to a classmate, telling someone what you liked about their work, making a Mother's Day card without prompting from Dad, picking up a piece of litter in the playground or inviting someone new to sit with you at lunchtime are all wonderful acts of kindness which will be very much appreciated by someone else.

Decluttering and having a tidy room makes us all feel good, plus it makes finding things much easier. If your child has a sort-out in their room, they might be able to put together a bag of items they have grown out of and which they could take to a charity shop. Even better, they may find something they no longer use which they could give to a friend or the younger sibling of someone they know. Old blankets and towels with plenty of life left in them could be donated to a local animal shelter.

If your child has any birthday money left over or they are lucky enough to get pocket money, there are schemes worldwide where you can buy a book for another child or sponsor a child so they can go to school. There is normally the opportunity for a two-way conversation with sponsorships. This may open up your child's eyes and benefit them by educating them about other cultures, countries and communities.

Sponsored walks, runs and cycle rides provide further opportunities for your child to be charitable. Some charities run volunteer schemes for young people, and bake sales and odd jobs for neighbours could raise money for your child's chosen charity as well. Not only will a charity benefit from your child's hard work, but your child's hormone systems will reward their bodies too. Along the way, they will encounter new people, broaden their experience of life and become a valuable member of society.

Jennie Segar

CLOSING WORDS

Thank you for giving your time to reading this book. I very much hope that you have found something here which will help you show your children how wonderful, strong and resilient they really are so that they can find true happiness in their lives.

References

H Highlight Strengths

List Strengths

1. Proctor, Carmel & Tsukayama, Eli & Wood, Alex & Maltby, John & Fox Eades, Jennifer & Linley, P.. (2011). Strengths Gym: The impact of a character strengths-based intervention on the life satisfaction and well-being of adolescents. *The Journal of Positive Psychology*. 6. 377-388. 10.1080/17439760.2011.594079.

2. Peterson, C., & Seligman, M. E. P. (2004). *Character strengths and virtues: A handbook and classification.* Oxford University Press; American Psychological Association.

Learn Gratitude

1. Bono, Giacomo & Krakauer, Mikki & Froh, Jeffrey. (2015). The Power and Practice of Gratitude. 10.1002/9781118996874.ch33.

2. Jeffrey J. Froh, Giacomo Bono, Jinyan Fan, Robert A. Emmons, Katherine Henderson, Cheray Harris, Heather Leggio & Alex M. Wood | Shannon Suldo (Associate Editor) (2014) Nice Thinking! An Educational Intervention That Teaches Children to

Think Gratefully, *School Psychology Review*, 43:2, 132-152, DOI: 10.1080/02796015.2014.12087440

Learn Optimism

1. Patton GC, Tollit MM, Romaniuk H, Spence SH, Sheffield J, Sawyer MG. A prospective study of the effects of optimism on adolescent health risks. Pediatrics. 2011 Feb;127(2):308-16. doi: 10.1542/peds.2010-0748. Epub 2011 Jan 10. PMID: 21220404.

2. Syed, Matthew. Black Box Thinking: The Surprising Truth About Success (and Why Most People Never Learn From Their Mistakes). New York: Portfolio/Penguin, 2015.

Use Self-Affirmations

1. Cascio CN, O'Donnell MB, Tinney FJ, Lieberman MD, Taylor SE, Strecher VJ, Falk EB. Self-affirmation activates brain systems associated with self-related processing and reward and is reinforced by future orientation. Soc Cogn Affect Neurosci. 2016 Apr;11(4):621-9. doi: 10.1093/scan/nsv136. Epub 2015 Nov 5. PMID: 26541373; PMCID: PMC4814782.

2. Cohen GL, Sherman DK. The psychology of change: self-affirmation and social psychological intervention. Annu Rev Psychol. 2014;65:333-71. doi: 10.1146/annurev-psych-010213-115137. PMID: 24405362.

3. Sherman, D. K., & Cohen, G. L. (2006). The psychology of self-defense: Self-affirmation theory. Advances in experimental social psychology, 38, 183-242.

4. Hadden IR, Easterbrook MJ, Nieuwenhuis M, Fox KJ, Dolan P. Self-affirmation reduces the socioeconomic attainment gap in schools in England. Br J Educ Psychol. 2020 May;90(2):517-536. doi: 10.1111/bjep.12291. Epub 2019 Jun 4. PMID: 31163515.

Learn Mindfulness

1. Dunning, D.L., Griffiths, K., Kuyken, W., Crane, C., Foulkes, L., Parker, J. and Dalgleish, T. (2019), Research Review: The effects of mindfulness-based interventions on cognition and mental health in children and adolescents – a meta-analysis of randomized controlled trials. J Child Psychol Psychiatr, 60: 244-258. https://doi.org/10.1111/jcpp.12980

2. Taren AA, Gianaros PJ, Greco CM, Lindsay EK, Fairgrieve A, Brown KW, Rosen RK, Ferris JL, Julson E, Marsland AL, Bursley JK, Ramsburg J, Creswell JD. Mindfulness meditation training alters stress-related amygdala resting state functional connectivity: a randomized controlled trial. Soc Cogn Affect Neurosci. 2015 Dec;10(12):1758-68. doi: 10.1093/scan/nsv066. Epub 2015 Jun 5. PMID: 26048176; PMCID: PMC4666115.

3. Weare, Katherine. "Evidence for the Impact of Mindfulness on Children and Young People." (2012).

4. Hőlzel, B. K., Carmody, J., Vangel, M., Congleton, C., Yerramsetti, S. M., Gard, T., & Lazar, S. W. (2011a). Mindfulness practice leads to increases in regional brain gray matter density. Psychiatry Research: Neuroimaging, 191, 36–43. doi:10.1016/j.psychresns.2010.08.006.

5. Amundsen, R., Riby, L.M., Hamilton, C. et al. Mindfulness in primary school children as a route to enhanced life satisfaction, positive outlook and effective emotion regulation. BMC Psychol 8, 71 (2020). https://doi.org/10.1186/s40359-020-00428-y

6. Weare K. (2018). The Evidence for Mindfulness in Schools for Children and Young People. Retrieved May 2023

Learn Forgiveness

1. Hui, E. K. P., & Chau, T. S. (2009). The impact of a forgiveness intervention with Hong Kong Chinese children hurt in interpersonal relationships. British Journal of Guidance & Counselling, 37(2), 141–156. https://doi.org/10.1080/03069880902728572

2. Rapp, H., Wang Xu, J., & Enright, R.D. (2022). A meta-analysis of forgiveness education interventions' effects on forgiveness and anger in children and adolescents. Child Development, 93, 1249–1269. https://doi.org/10.1111/cdev.13771

3. Waldinger, R. (2002). The study of adult development. United States of America. Fonte: http://hr1973. org/docs/Harvard35thReunion_Waldinger. pdf.

Journal Regularly

1. Pennebaker JW. Expressive Writing in Psychological Science. Perspect Psychol Sci. 2018 Mar;13(2):226-229. doi: 10.1177/1745691617707315. Epub 2017 Oct 9. PMID: 28992443.

2. Smyth JM, Johnson JA, Auer BJ, Lehman E, Talamo G, Sciamanna CN. Online Positive Affect Journaling in the Improvement of Mental Distress and Well-Being in General Medical Patients With Elevated Anxiety Symptoms: A Preliminary Randomized Controlled Trial. JMIR Ment Health. 2018 Dec 10;5(4):e11290. doi: 10.2196/11290. PMID: 30530460; PMCID: PMC6305886.

3. Lieberman MD, Eisenberger NI, Crockett MJ, Tom SM, Pfeifer JH, Way BM. Putting feelings into words: affect labeling disrupts amygdala activity in response to affective stimuli. Psychol Sci. 2007 May;18(5):421-8. doi: 10.1111/j.1467-9280.2007.01916.x. PMID: 17576282.

4. Lara, Lauren. (2020). Benefits of journal-writing for students in the emotional/behavior disorders classroom. Journal of Poetry Therapy. 33. 1-7. 10.1080/08893675.2020.1776971.

U Understand Difficult Topics

Drugs, Smoking and Alcohol

1. Louise Ann Rohrbach, Carol S. Hodgson, Benjamin I. Broder, Susan B. Montgomery, Brian R. Flay, William B. Hansen & Mary Ann Pentz (1994) Parental Participation in Drug Abuse Prevention: Results From the Midwestern Prevention Project, Journal of Research on Adolescence, 4:2, 295-317,
DOI: 10.1207/s15327795jra0402_7

2. Hannah Carver, Lawrie Elliott, Catriona Kennedy & Janet Hanley (2017) Parent–child connectedness and communication in relation to alcohol, tobacco and drug use in adolescence: An integrative review of the literature, Drugs: Education, Prevention and Policy, 24:2, 119-133,

DOI: 10.1080/09687637.2016.1221060

Sex Education

1. Pennebaker, James. (2017). Expressive Writing in Psychological Science. Perspectives on Psychological Science. 13. 174569161770731. 10.1177/1745691617707315.

2. Turnbull, T., Van Wersch, A., & Van Schaik, P. (2008). A review of parental involvement in sex education: The role for effective communication in British families. Health Education Journal, 67(3), 182-195.

3. Widman L, Choukas-Bradley S, Noar SM, Nesi J, Garrett K. Parent-Adolescent Sexual Communication and Adolescent Safer Sex Behavior: A Meta-Analysis. JAMA Pediatr. 2016;170(1):52–61. doi:10.1001/jamapediatrics.2015.2731

Online Safety and Social Media

1. Dyer, Tobbi. (2018). The Effects of Social Media on Children. Dalhousie Journal of Interdisciplinary Management. 14. 10.5931/djim.v14i0.7855.

2. Sun, X., Haydel, K. F., Matheson, D., Desai, M., & Robinson, T. N. (2023). Are mobile phone ownership and age of acquisition associated with child adjustment? A 5-year prospective study among low-income Latinx children. Child Development, 94, 303– 314. https://doi.org/10.1111/cdev.13851

3. Fox, J. (2018). An unlikeable truth: Social media like buttons are designed to be addictive. They're impacting our ability to think rationally. Index on Censorship, 47(3), 11-13.

4. Fardouly, J., & Vartanian, L. R. (2016). Social media and body image concerns: Current research and future directions. Current opinion in psychology, 9, 1-5.

Bullying

1. Committee on the Biological and Psychosocial Effects of Peer Victimization: Lessons for Bullying Prevention; Board on

Children, Youth, and Families; Committee on Law and Justice; Division of Behavioral and Social Sciences and Education; Health and Medicine Division; National Academies of Sciences, Engineering, and Medicine. Preventing Bullying Through Science, Policy, and Practice. Rivara F, Le Menestrel S, editors. Washington (DC): National Academies Press (US); 2016 Sep 14. PMID: 27748087.

2. Richard Long, Nerys Roberts, Philip Loft (2020) Bullying in UK Schools, House of Commons Library Briefing Paper

3. Wolke, D., & Lereya, S. T. (2015). Long-term effects of bullying. Archives of disease in childhood, 100(9), 879-885.

4. Marinoff, L (2004) The big questions: how philosophy can change your life. London, Bloomsbury

Difficult Truths

1. Coley RL, Kull M. Cumulative, Timing-Specific, and Interactive Models of Residential Mobility and Children's Cognitive and Psychosocial Skills. Child Dev. 2016 Jul;87(4):1204-20. doi: 10.1111/cdev.12535. Epub 2016 May 25. PMID: 27223111.

2. D'Onofrio B, Emery R. Parental divorce or separation and children's mental health. World Psychiatry. 2019 Feb;18(1):100-

101. doi: 10.1002/wps.20590. PMID: 30600636; PMCID: PMC6313686.

3. Mazrekaj, D., De Witte, K., & Cabus, S. (2020). School Outcomes of Children Raised by Same-Sex Parents: Evidence from Administrative Panel Data. American Sociological Review, 85(5), 830–856. https://doi.org/10.1177/0003122420957249

4. Fagan, P. F., & Churchill, A. (2012). The effects of divorce on children. Marri Research, 1, 1-48.

5. Brent DA, Melhem NM, Masten AS, Porta G, Payne MW. Longitudinal effects of parental bereavement on adolescent developmental competence. J Clin Child Adolesc Psychol. 2012;41(6):778-91. doi: 10.1080/15374416.2012.717871. Epub 2012 Sep 25. PMID: 23009724; PMCID: PMC3493857.

G Gather your Happiness

1. Shahnazi M, Nikjoo R, Yavarikia P, Mohammad-Alizadeh-Charandabi S. Inhaled lavender effect on anxiety and pain caused from intrauterine device insertion. J Caring Sci. 2012 Nov 28;1(4):255-61. doi: 10.5681/jcs.2012.035. PMID: 25276703; PMCID: PMC4161086.

2. Dfarhud D, Malmir M, Khanahmadi M. Happiness & Health: The Biological Factors- Systematic Review Article. Iran J Public

Health. 2014 Nov;43(11):1468-77. PMID: 26060713; PMCID: PMC4449495.

Printed in Great Britain
by Amazon

38275539R00086